50 Holiday Baking Recipes for Home

By: Kelly Johnson

Table of Contents

- Toffee Crunch Bars
- Spiced Nuts
- Holiday Thumbprint Cookies
- Dark Chocolate Cranberry Tart
- Cinnamon Roll Casserole
- Peppermint Mocha Brownies
- Fig and Walnut Cookies
- Classic Fruit and Nut Cake
- Apple Streusel Bars
- Chocolate Mint Pie
- Raspberry Almond Bars
- Poppy Seed Loaf
- Hazelnut Coffee Cake
- Eggnog Macarons

Gingerbread Cookies

Ingredients:

- **Dry Ingredients:**
    - 3 1/4 cups all-purpose flour
    - 1/4 teaspoon baking powder
    - 1/2 teaspoon baking soda
    - 1 tablespoon ground ginger
    - 1 tablespoon ground cinnamon
    - 1/2 teaspoon ground cloves
    - 1/4 teaspoon salt
- **Wet Ingredients:**
    - 1/2 cup (1 stick) unsalted butter, room temperature
    - 1/2 cup granulated sugar
    - 1/2 cup packed brown sugar
    - 1 large egg
    - 1/2 cup molasses (not blackstrap)
- **For the Royal Icing (Optional for Decorating):**
    - 2 large egg whites
    - 4 cups powdered sugar
    - 1/2 teaspoon lemon juice or vinegar

Instructions:

1. **Preheat Oven:**
    - Preheat your oven to 350°F (175°C). Line baking sheets with parchment paper or silicone baking mats.
2. **Mix Dry Ingredients:**
    - In a medium bowl, whisk together flour, baking powder, baking soda, ginger, cinnamon, cloves, and salt. Set aside.
3. **Cream Butter and Sugars:**
    - In a large bowl, use an electric mixer to cream together the butter, granulated sugar, and brown sugar until light and fluffy, about 2-3 minutes.
4. **Add Egg and Molasses:**
    - Beat in the egg until well combined. Mix in the molasses until smooth.
5. **Combine Wet and Dry Ingredients:**
    - Gradually add the dry ingredients to the wet ingredients, mixing just until combined. The dough will be thick.
6. **Roll Out Dough:**
    - Divide the dough into two portions and roll out each portion on a lightly floured surface to about 1/4-inch thickness.
7. **Cut Out Cookies:**

- Use cookie cutters to cut out shapes and transfer them to the prepared baking sheets. If you want to hang them as ornaments, use a straw to make a hole at the top before baking.

8. **Bake:**
   - Bake in the preheated oven for 8-10 minutes, or until the edges are firm and slightly darker. The centers may look soft but will firm up as they cool.

9. **Cool:**
   - Allow the cookies to cool on the baking sheets for about 5 minutes before transferring them to a wire rack to cool completely.

10. **Decorate (Optional):**
    - To make royal icing, beat the egg whites with a mixer until frothy. Gradually add powdered sugar and lemon juice or vinegar, beating until the mixture forms stiff peaks. Decorate the cookies as desired, then let the icing dry completely.

Tips:

- **Chilling Dough:** If the dough is too soft to roll out, chill it in the refrigerator for about 30 minutes.
- **Cutting Shapes:** Use lightly floured cookie cutters to prevent the dough from sticking. For more intricate designs, consider using a piping bag for detailed decoration.
- **Storing Cookies:** Store the cookies in an airtight container at room temperature for up to a week. They also freeze well for longer storage.

Enjoy your Gingerbread Cookies! They are a festive and fun treat that's perfect for holiday gatherings and cookie decorating.

Peppermint Bark

Ingredients:

- **For the Bark:**
    - 12 ounces semisweet chocolate (chopped or in chips)
    - 12 ounces white chocolate (chopped or in chips)
    - 1 teaspoon peppermint extract
    - 1/2 cup crushed peppermint candies or candy canes

Instructions:

1. **Prepare Pan:**
    - Line a baking sheet with parchment paper or a silicone baking mat. Set aside.
2. **Melt Semisweet Chocolate:**
    - In a heatproof bowl, melt the semisweet chocolate over a pot of simmering water (double boiler method), stirring occasionally until smooth. Alternatively, you can melt the chocolate in the microwave in 30-second intervals, stirring after each interval, until fully melted.
3. **Spread Semisweet Chocolate:**
    - Pour the melted semisweet chocolate onto the prepared baking sheet. Use a spatula to spread it into an even layer about 1/4 inch thick. Place the baking sheet in the refrigerator for about 20 minutes, or until the chocolate is set.
4. **Melt White Chocolate:**
    - While the semisweet chocolate is setting, melt the white chocolate using the same method as before (double boiler or microwave). Stir in the peppermint extract.
5. **Spread White Chocolate:**
    - Once the semisweet chocolate is set, pour the melted white chocolate over the top. Use a spatula to spread it evenly over the semisweet layer.
6. **Add Peppermint Candies:**
    - Sprinkle the crushed peppermint candies evenly over the white chocolate layer while it is still soft. Press the candies down lightly into the chocolate.
7. **Chill:**
    - Return the baking sheet to the refrigerator and chill until the bark is completely set and hardened, about 1 hour.
8. **Break into Pieces:**
    - Once the bark is set, break it into pieces of varying sizes.

Tips:

- **Crushing Peppermints:** To crush peppermint candies or candy canes, place them in a plastic bag and gently crush them with a rolling pin or the bottom of a heavy pan.

- **Melting Chocolate:** Ensure no water gets into the chocolate while melting, as even a small amount of water can cause the chocolate to seize up.
- **Storing:** Store the peppermint bark in an airtight container at room temperature for up to 2 weeks. You can also freeze it for longer storage; just be sure to keep it in a well-sealed container to avoid freezer burn.

Enjoy your Peppermint Bark! It's a delightful holiday treat that combines the richness of chocolate with the refreshing crunch of peppermint.

Eggnog Cheesecake

Ingredients:

- **For the Crust:**
    - 1 1/2 cups graham cracker crumbs
    - 1/4 cup granulated sugar
    - 1/2 cup (1 stick) unsalted butter, melted
- **For the Filling:**
    - 4 packages (8 ounces each) cream cheese, softened
    - 1 cup granulated sugar
    - 1 cup eggnog
    - 3 large eggs
    - 1 teaspoon vanilla extract
    - 1/2 teaspoon ground nutmeg
    - 1/4 teaspoon ground cinnamon
- **For the Topping (Optional):**
    - Whipped cream
    - Ground nutmeg for garnish

Instructions:

1. **Preheat Oven:**
    - Preheat your oven to 325°F (163°C).
2. **Prepare the Crust:**
    - In a medium bowl, combine the graham cracker crumbs, granulated sugar, and melted butter. Stir until the mixture resembles wet sand.
    - Press the mixture evenly into the bottom of a 9-inch springform pan. Use the back of a spoon or the bottom of a glass to press it down firmly.
3. **Bake the Crust:**
    - Bake the crust in the preheated oven for 8-10 minutes, or until lightly golden. Remove from the oven and set aside to cool.
4. **Prepare the Filling:**
    - In a large bowl, beat the softened cream cheese with an electric mixer until smooth and creamy.
    - Gradually add the granulated sugar, beating until well combined.
    - Add the eggnog, vanilla extract, ground nutmeg, and ground cinnamon. Mix until smooth.
    - Add the eggs one at a time, beating just until combined after each addition. Do not overmix.
5. **Bake the Cheesecake:**
    - Pour the cream cheese mixture over the cooled crust in the springform pan.

- Bake in the preheated oven for 50-60 minutes, or until the center is set and the edges are lightly golden. The cheesecake should have a slight jiggle in the center.
- Turn off the oven, crack the oven door slightly, and let the cheesecake cool in the oven for 1 hour to prevent cracking.

6. **Chill:**
   - After cooling in the oven, remove the cheesecake from the oven and refrigerate for at least 4 hours, or overnight, to fully set and develop flavor.

7. **Serve:**
   - Before serving, top with whipped cream and a sprinkle of ground nutmeg if desired.

Tips:

- **Cream Cheese:** Make sure the cream cheese is softened to room temperature to avoid lumps in the filling.
- **Crack-Free Cheesecake:** To minimize the risk of cracks, avoid overmixing the batter and ensure the cheesecake cools gradually in the oven.
- **Flavor:** If you prefer a stronger eggnog flavor, you can increase the amount of eggnog slightly, but be cautious not to make the filling too liquid.

Enjoy your Eggnog Cheesecake! It's a rich, festive dessert that's sure to impress your guests during the holiday season.

Sugar Cookies with Royal Icing

Ingredients:

For the Sugar Cookies:

- **Dry Ingredients:**
    - 3 1/4 cups all-purpose flour
    - 1/2 teaspoon baking powder
    - 1/2 teaspoon salt
- **Wet Ingredients:**
    - 1 cup (2 sticks) unsalted butter, room temperature
    - 1 1/2 cups granulated sugar
    - 1 large egg
    - 1 teaspoon vanilla extract

For the Royal Icing:

- 2 large egg whites (or use meringue powder if you prefer)
- 4 cups powdered sugar, sifted
- 1/2 teaspoon lemon juice or vinegar
- Food coloring (optional)

Instructions:

1. Prepare the Sugar Cookies:

1. **Preheat Oven:**
    - Preheat your oven to 350°F (175°C). Line baking sheets with parchment paper or silicone baking mats.
2. **Mix Dry Ingredients:**
    - In a medium bowl, whisk together the flour, baking powder, and salt. Set aside.
3. **Cream Butter and Sugar:**
    - In a large bowl, use an electric mixer to cream together the butter and granulated sugar until light and fluffy, about 2-3 minutes.
4. **Add Egg and Vanilla:**
    - Beat in the egg until fully incorporated. Mix in the vanilla extract until smooth.
5. **Combine Wet and Dry Ingredients:**
    - Gradually add the dry ingredients to the wet ingredients, mixing just until combined. The dough will be thick.
6. **Roll Out Dough:**
    - Divide the dough into two portions. On a lightly floured surface, roll out one portion of dough to about 1/4-inch thickness.
7. **Cut Out Cookies:**

- Use cookie cutters to cut out shapes and transfer them to the prepared baking sheets.
8. **Bake:**
   - Bake in the preheated oven for 8-10 minutes, or until the edges are lightly golden. The centers may look soft but will firm up as they cool.
9. **Cool:**
   - Allow the cookies to cool on the baking sheets for about 5 minutes before transferring them to a wire rack to cool completely.

2. Prepare the Royal Icing:

1. **Beat Egg Whites:**
   - In a large bowl, beat the egg whites until frothy. If using meringue powder, follow the instructions on the package to substitute for egg whites.
2. **Add Powdered Sugar:**
   - Gradually add the sifted powdered sugar to the egg whites, beating until the mixture forms stiff peaks.
3. **Add Lemon Juice/Vinegar:**
   - Mix in the lemon juice or vinegar. This helps stabilize the icing and adds a bit of shine.
4. **Divide and Color (Optional):**
   - If using multiple colors, divide the icing into separate bowls and add food coloring as desired. Mix until the color is evenly distributed.
5. **Consistency:**
   - Adjust the consistency by adding a few drops of water to thin it or additional powdered sugar to thicken it, depending on the design you plan to create. For outlining, the icing should be thick; for flooding, it should be slightly thinner.

3. Decorate the Cookies:

1. **Outline Cookies:**
   - Using a piping bag fitted with a small round tip, pipe the outline of each cookie. Let it dry for about 15-30 minutes.
2. **Flood Cookies:**
   - Once the outlines are dry, use a slightly thinned icing to fill in the centers of the cookies. Use a toothpick or small spatula to spread the icing evenly and to pop any air bubbles.
3. **Add Details:**
   - Allow the base layer of icing to dry completely before adding any additional details or decorations.
4. **Dry Completely:**
   - Let the decorated cookies dry for at least 24 hours to ensure the icing is fully set and hard before stacking or packaging.

Tips:

- **Chilling Dough:** If the dough is too soft to work with, chill it in the refrigerator for about 30 minutes before rolling it out.
- **Icing Tips:** Keep the royal icing covered with a damp cloth to prevent it from drying out while working with it.
- **Storage:** Store decorated cookies in an airtight container at room temperature. They can be kept for up to a week, but the texture and design may last longer if the cookies are stored properly.

Enjoy decorating and eating your Sugar Cookies with Royal Icing! They make a delightful treat and a fun activity for the holiday season or any special occasion.

Cranberry Orange Bread

Ingredients:

- **For the Bread:**
    - 2 cups all-purpose flour
    - 1 cup granulated sugar
    - 1 1/2 teaspoons baking powder
    - 1/2 teaspoon baking soda
    - 1/2 teaspoon salt
    - 1/2 teaspoon ground cinnamon (optional)
    - 1/2 cup (1 stick) unsalted butter, melted
    - 1/2 cup orange juice (freshly squeezed is best)
    - 2 large eggs
    - 1 tablespoon grated orange zest (about 1 orange)
    - 1 1/2 cups fresh or frozen cranberries (if using frozen, do not thaw)
- **For the Glaze (Optional):**
    - 1/2 cup powdered sugar
    - 2 tablespoons orange juice
    - 1/2 teaspoon grated orange zest

Instructions:

1. **Preheat Oven:**
    - Preheat your oven to 350°F (175°C). Grease and flour a 9x5-inch loaf pan, or line it with parchment paper.
2. **Mix Dry Ingredients:**
    - In a medium bowl, whisk together the flour, granulated sugar, baking powder, baking soda, salt, and cinnamon (if using). Set aside.
3. **Combine Wet Ingredients:**
    - In a large bowl, whisk together the melted butter, orange juice, eggs, and grated orange zest until well combined.
4. **Mix Wet and Dry Ingredients:**
    - Gradually add the dry ingredients to the wet ingredients, mixing just until combined. Do not overmix. The batter will be thick.
5. **Fold in Cranberries:**
    - Gently fold in the cranberries until evenly distributed throughout the batter.
6. **Pour Batter into Pan:**
    - Pour the batter into the prepared loaf pan, spreading it evenly.
7. **Bake:**
    - Bake in the preheated oven for 55-65 minutes, or until a toothpick inserted into the center of the bread comes out clean. The top should be golden brown.
8. **Cool:**

- Allow the bread to cool in the pan for about 10 minutes, then transfer it to a wire rack to cool completely.

9. **Prepare the Glaze (Optional):**
   - While the bread is cooling, mix the powdered sugar, orange juice, and grated orange zest in a small bowl until smooth. Drizzle over the cooled bread if desired.

Tips:

- **Cranberries:** If using fresh cranberries, be sure to chop them roughly to prevent them from sinking to the bottom. If using frozen cranberries, toss them with a bit of flour before adding them to the batter to help distribute them more evenly.
- **Overmixing:** Be careful not to overmix the batter, as this can lead to a dense loaf.
- **Storage:** Store the bread in an airtight container at room temperature for up to 4 days. It can also be frozen for up to 3 months; just wrap it tightly in plastic wrap and foil before freezing.

Enjoy your Cranberry Orange Bread! It's a delightful and festive treat that's sure to impress.

Pecan Pie Bars

Ingredients:

For the Crust:

- 1 1/2 cups all-purpose flour
- 1/4 cup granulated sugar
- 1/2 teaspoon salt
- 1/2 cup (1 stick) unsalted butter, cold and cut into small pieces

For the Filling:

- 1 cup light brown sugar, packed
- 1/2 cup corn syrup (light or dark)
- 1/4 cup unsalted butter, melted
- 2 large eggs
- 1 teaspoon vanilla extract
- 1 1/2 cups chopped pecans

Instructions:

1. **Preheat Oven:**
   - Preheat your oven to 350°F (175°C). Grease or line an 8x8-inch baking pan with parchment paper, leaving an overhang on the sides for easy removal.
2. **Prepare the Crust:**
   - In a medium bowl, combine the flour, granulated sugar, and salt. Cut in the cold butter using a pastry cutter or your fingers until the mixture resembles coarse crumbs.
   - Press the mixture evenly into the bottom of the prepared baking pan to form a smooth layer.
3. **Bake the Crust:**
   - Bake in the preheated oven for 15-20 minutes, or until the crust is lightly golden. Remove from the oven and let it cool slightly while you prepare the filling.
4. **Prepare the Filling:**
   - In a large bowl, whisk together the brown sugar, corn syrup, melted butter, eggs, and vanilla extract until well combined.
   - Stir in the chopped pecans.
5. **Assemble the Bars:**
   - Pour the pecan filling evenly over the partially baked crust.
6. **Bake:**
   - Bake in the preheated oven for 25-30 minutes, or until the filling is set and the top is golden brown. A toothpick inserted into the center should come out with just a few moist crumbs.
7. **Cool:**

- Allow the bars to cool completely in the pan on a wire rack. Once cooled, lift the bars out of the pan using the parchment paper overhang and cut into squares.

Tips:

- **Crust Texture:** Make sure the butter is cold when cutting it into the flour for the crust to ensure a flaky texture.
- **Pecan Size:** Chop the pecans to your desired size; smaller pieces will distribute more evenly throughout the filling.
- **Storage:** Store the bars in an airtight container at room temperature for up to a week. They can also be refrigerated for longer storage.

Enjoy your Pecan Pie Bars! They offer the rich, nutty flavor of traditional pecan pie with the convenience of a bar format, perfect for sharing and enjoying throughout the holiday season or any time of year.

Chocolate Peppermint Cupcakes

Ingredients

For the Cupcakes:

- 1 ¼ cups all-purpose flour
- ¾ cup unsweetened cocoa powder
- 1 cup granulated sugar
- 1 tsp baking powder
- ½ tsp baking soda
- ½ tsp salt
- ½ cup vegetable oil
- 2 large eggs
- 1 cup buttermilk
- 1 tsp vanilla extract
- ½ tsp peppermint extract

For the Peppermint Frosting:

- ½ cup unsalted butter, softened
- 2 cups powdered sugar
- 2 tbsp heavy cream
- 1 tsp vanilla extract
- ½ tsp peppermint extract
- Crushed peppermint candies (optional, for garnish)

Instructions

1. Preheat the Oven:

- Preheat your oven to 350°F (175°C). Line a muffin tin with paper liners.

2. Prepare the Cupcake Batter:

- In a medium bowl, whisk together the flour, cocoa powder, sugar, baking powder, baking soda, and salt.
- In another bowl, combine the oil, eggs, buttermilk, vanilla extract, and peppermint extract.
- Gradually add the wet ingredients to the dry ingredients, mixing until just combined.

3. Bake the Cupcakes:

- Divide the batter evenly among the cupcake liners, filling each about 2/3 full.
- Bake for 18-20 minutes, or until a toothpick inserted into the center comes out clean.

- Allow the cupcakes to cool in the tin for 5 minutes, then transfer them to a wire rack to cool completely.

4. Prepare the Frosting:

- Beat the softened butter in a bowl until creamy.
- Gradually add the powdered sugar, beating well after each addition.
- Add the heavy cream, vanilla extract, and peppermint extract. Continue to beat until the frosting is light and fluffy.

5. Frost the Cupcakes:

- Once the cupcakes are completely cooled, frost them with the peppermint frosting.
- Garnish with crushed peppermint candies if desired.

Enjoy your festive and flavorful chocolate peppermint cupcakes! They're perfect for the holidays or any time you need a minty chocolate treat.

Pumpkin Spice Muffins

Ingredients

For the Muffins:

- 1 ¾ cups all-purpose flour
- 1 cup granulated sugar
- 1 tsp baking powder
- 1 tsp baking soda
- 1 tsp ground cinnamon
- ½ tsp ground nutmeg
- ½ tsp ground ginger
- ½ tsp salt
- 1 cup canned pumpkin puree (not pumpkin pie filling)
- ½ cup vegetable oil
- 2 large eggs
- ¼ cup milk (whole or 2%)
- 1 tsp vanilla extract

For the Optional Streusel Topping:

- ¼ cup granulated sugar
- ¼ cup all-purpose flour
- ¼ cup cold unsalted butter, cut into small pieces
- 1 tsp ground cinnamon

Instructions

1. Preheat the Oven:

- Preheat your oven to 375°F (190°C). Line a muffin tin with paper liners or lightly grease it.

2. Prepare the Muffin Batter:

- In a large bowl, whisk together the flour, sugar, baking powder, baking soda, cinnamon, nutmeg, ginger, and salt.
- In another bowl, mix the pumpkin puree, vegetable oil, eggs, milk, and vanilla extract until well combined.
- Gradually add the wet ingredients to the dry ingredients, stirring just until combined. Be careful not to overmix.

3. Prepare the Streusel Topping (Optional):

- In a small bowl, combine the sugar, flour, cinnamon, and cold butter.

- Use a fork or pastry cutter to cut the butter into the mixture until it resembles coarse crumbs.

4. Fill the Muffin Tin:

- Divide the batter evenly among the muffin cups, filling each about 2/3 full.
- If using the streusel topping, sprinkle it generously over each muffin.

5. Bake the Muffins:

- Bake for 18-22 minutes, or until a toothpick inserted into the center comes out clean.
- Allow the muffins to cool in the tin for about 5 minutes before transferring them to a wire rack to cool completely.

Enjoy your pumpkin spice muffins with a cup of coffee or tea! They're perfect for fall and will fill your kitchen with a delightful aroma.

Apple Cinnamon Rolls

Ingredients

For the Dough:

- 1 cup whole milk, warmed to 110°F (45°C)
- ¼ cup granulated sugar
- 2 ¼ tsp (1 packet) active dry yeast
- ¼ cup unsalted butter, melted
- 1 large egg
- 3 ½ to 4 cups all-purpose flour
- ½ tsp salt

For the Apple Filling:

- 2 large apples (Granny Smith or Honeycrisp), peeled, cored, and finely chopped
- ¼ cup granulated sugar
- 1 tsp ground cinnamon
- 2 tbsp unsalted butter, melted

For the Cream Cheese Glaze:

- 4 oz cream cheese, softened
- 2 tbsp unsalted butter, softened
- 1 ½ cups powdered sugar
- 1 tsp vanilla extract
- 1-2 tbsp milk (as needed for consistency)

Instructions

1. Prepare the Dough:

- In a small bowl, combine the warm milk and sugar. Stir to dissolve, then sprinkle the yeast over the top. Let it sit for about 5 minutes, or until frothy.
- In a large bowl or the bowl of a stand mixer, combine 3 ½ cups flour and salt. Make a well in the center and add the yeast mixture, melted butter, and egg. Mix until a dough forms.
- If using a stand mixer, knead the dough with the dough hook attachment on low speed for about 5-7 minutes, adding more flour if needed. If kneading by hand, turn the dough onto a floured surface and knead for 8-10 minutes.
- The dough should be smooth and elastic. Place it in a lightly oiled bowl, cover with a damp cloth, and let it rise in a warm place for about 1-1.5 hours, or until doubled in size.

2. Prepare the Apple Filling:

- In a medium bowl, toss the chopped apples with sugar and cinnamon. Set aside.

3. Roll Out the Dough:

- Punch down the risen dough and turn it out onto a floured surface. Roll it out into a rectangle about 14x10 inches.

4. Assemble the Rolls:

- Brush the melted butter over the rolled-out dough.
- Evenly sprinkle the apple mixture over the dough.
- Starting from one long side, tightly roll the dough into a log. Pinch the seam to seal.
- Slice the log into 12 even pieces and place them in a greased 9x13-inch baking dish or two 8-inch round pans.

5. Second Rise:

- Cover the rolls with a damp cloth or plastic wrap and let them rise for about 30 minutes, or until puffy.

6. Bake the Rolls:

- Preheat your oven to 350°F (175°C).
- Bake the rolls for 25-30 minutes, or until golden brown. If they start to brown too quickly, you can cover them loosely with foil.

7. Prepare the Cream Cheese Glaze:

- While the rolls are baking, beat together the cream cheese, butter, powdered sugar, vanilla extract, and milk until smooth. Adjust the milk as needed to reach your desired consistency.

8. Glaze the Rolls:

- Let the rolls cool slightly before drizzling with the cream cheese glaze.

Enjoy these warm, gooey apple cinnamon rolls with a cup of coffee or tea! They're perfect for a special breakfast or a delightful dessert.

Sticky Toffee Pudding

Ingredients

For the Pudding:

- 1 cup (200g) pitted dates, chopped
- 1 tsp baking soda
- 1 cup (240ml) boiling water
- ½ cup (115g) unsalted butter, softened
- ½ cup (100g) granulated sugar
- ¼ cup (50g) packed brown sugar
- 2 large eggs
- 1 tsp vanilla extract
- 1 ½ cups (190g) all-purpose flour
- 1 ½ tsp baking powder
- ¼ tsp salt

For the Toffee Sauce:

- ½ cup (115g) unsalted butter
- 1 cup (200g) packed brown sugar
- ½ cup (120ml) heavy cream
- 1 tbsp light corn syrup (optional, but helps prevent crystallization)
- ½ tsp vanilla extract

Instructions

1. Prepare the Pudding:

- Preheat your oven to 350°F (175°C). Grease a 9x9-inch (23x23 cm) baking dish or a similar-sized ovenproof dish.
- In a medium bowl, combine the chopped dates and baking soda. Pour the boiling water over the dates and let them soak for about 10 minutes. Then mash the dates with a fork or a potato masher until smooth.

2. Make the Pudding Batter:

- In a large bowl, cream together the softened butter, granulated sugar, and brown sugar until light and fluffy.
- Beat in the eggs one at a time, then add the vanilla extract.
- In a separate bowl, sift together the flour, baking powder, and salt.
- Gradually add the dry ingredients to the wet mixture, alternating with the date mixture. Mix until just combined.

3. Bake the Pudding:

- Pour the batter into the prepared baking dish and smooth the top.
- Bake for 30-35 minutes, or until a toothpick inserted into the center comes out clean. The pudding should be firm to the touch but still soft and moist in the center.

4. Prepare the Toffee Sauce:

- While the pudding is baking, make the toffee sauce. In a medium saucepan, melt the butter over medium heat.
- Stir in the brown sugar and cook, stirring frequently, until the sugar is dissolved and the mixture starts to boil.
- Reduce the heat and simmer for about 2-3 minutes, then slowly stir in the heavy cream. Continue to cook, stirring, for another 2-3 minutes, or until the sauce is smooth and slightly thickened.
- Remove from heat and stir in the vanilla extract. If using corn syrup, add it here to help prevent crystallization.

5. Serve the Pudding:

- Once the pudding is done, remove it from the oven and let it cool for about 10 minutes.
- Cut the pudding into squares and serve warm with the toffee sauce drizzled over the top. You can also serve it with a scoop of vanilla ice cream or a dollop of whipped cream if desired.

Enjoy your sticky toffee pudding! It's a comforting and decadent dessert that's sure to be a hit.

Yule Log Cake

Ingredients

For the Sponge Cake:

- 4 large eggs, separated
- ⅔ cup (130g) granulated sugar
- ⅓ cup (40g) all-purpose flour
- ⅓ cup (40g) unsweetened cocoa powder
- ¼ tsp salt
- 1 tsp vanilla extract
- 1 tsp baking powder

For the Filling:

- 1 cup (240ml) heavy cream
- 2 tbsp powdered sugar
- 1 tsp vanilla extract

For the Chocolate Ganache:

- 8 oz (225g) semisweet chocolate, chopped
- 1 cup (240ml) heavy cream
- 2 tbsp unsalted butter (optional, for extra gloss)

For Decoration (optional):

- Powdered sugar, for dusting
- Fresh berries or edible flowers

Instructions

1. Prepare the Sponge Cake:

- Preheat your oven to 375°F (190°C). Line a 15x10-inch (38x25 cm) jelly roll pan or a similar-sized baking sheet with parchment paper.
- In a large bowl, beat the egg yolks with ⅓ cup of sugar until pale and thick. Mix in the vanilla extract.
- In a separate bowl, sift together the flour, cocoa powder, salt, and baking powder.
- Gently fold the dry ingredients into the egg yolk mixture until combined.
- In another bowl, beat the egg whites until soft peaks form. Gradually add the remaining ⅓ cup sugar and continue to beat until stiff peaks form.
- Fold the egg whites into the batter in three additions, being careful not to deflate the mixture.

- Spread the batter evenly in the prepared pan and bake for 10-12 minutes, or until the cake springs back when touched.

2. Roll the Cake:

- While the cake is baking, lay out a clean kitchen towel on a flat surface and dust it with powdered sugar.
- Once the cake is done, immediately invert it onto the prepared towel and peel off the parchment paper.
- Starting at one end, carefully roll the cake up with the towel. Let it cool completely while rolled up.

3. Prepare the Filling:

- In a medium bowl, whip the heavy cream with powdered sugar and vanilla extract until stiff peaks form.
- Once the cake is cool, gently unroll it and spread the whipped cream evenly over the surface.

4. Roll the Cake Again:

- Re-roll the cake without the towel, using the filling as the "glue" to hold it together.
- Place the rolled cake seam-side down on a serving platter.

5. Prepare the Ganache:

- In a saucepan, heat the heavy cream until it just begins to simmer. Pour it over the chopped chocolate in a heatproof bowl.
- Let it sit for 2-3 minutes, then stir until smooth. If desired, add the butter for extra gloss and richness.
- Allow the ganache to cool slightly until it thickens to a spreadable consistency.

6. Frost the Cake:

- Spread the ganache evenly over the rolled cake, using a spatula to create a bark-like texture if desired.
- For added decoration, dust the cake with powdered sugar and garnish with fresh berries or edible flowers.

7. Serve:

- Chill the cake for at least 30 minutes to set the ganache before slicing and serving.

Enjoy your festive Yule log cake! It's a beautiful and delicious centerpiece for your holiday celebrations.

Chocolate Dipped Pretzels

Ingredients

- 1 bag (16 oz) pretzel rods or mini pretzels (sticks or twists)
- 1 cup semi-sweet chocolate chips or coarsely chopped chocolate
- 1 cup white chocolate chips (optional, for drizzling)
- Sprinkles, crushed nuts, or crushed candy canes (optional, for decoration)

Instructions

1. Prepare Your Workspace:

- Line a baking sheet with parchment paper or wax paper to catch any drips and make cleanup easier.

2. Melt the Chocolate:

- **For Semi-Sweet Chocolate:**
  - Place the semi-sweet chocolate chips in a microwave-safe bowl.
  - Heat in the microwave in 30-second intervals, stirring in between, until completely melted and smooth.
- **For White Chocolate (if using):**
  - Place the white chocolate chips in a separate microwave-safe bowl.
  - Heat in the microwave in 30-second intervals, stirring in between, until melted and smooth.

3. Dip the Pretzels:

- Hold each pretzel by one end and dip it into the melted chocolate, covering about half to three-quarters of the pretzel.
- Allow any excess chocolate to drip off before placing the pretzel on the prepared baking sheet.

4. Add Decorations (Optional):

- If using sprinkles, crushed nuts, or crushed candy canes, sprinkle them over the chocolate-dipped portion while the chocolate is still wet.
- If using white chocolate for drizzling, use a fork or spoon to drizzle the white chocolate over the dipped pretzels in a zigzag pattern. Allow the white chocolate to set before proceeding with more decorations.

5. Let the Chocolate Set:

- Allow the dipped pretzels to sit at room temperature until the chocolate is fully set, which usually takes about 30 minutes to an hour.

- For quicker setting, you can place the baking sheet in the refrigerator for about 15-20 minutes.

6. Store:

- Once the chocolate is set, store the pretzels in an airtight container at room temperature for up to 2 weeks.

Enjoy these chocolate-dipped pretzels as a sweet and salty snack or as a charming homemade gift! They're versatile and can be customized with various toppings to suit your taste.

Eggnog Cupcakes

Ingredients

For the Cupcakes:

- 1 ½ cups all-purpose flour
- 1 ½ tsp baking powder
- ¼ tsp baking soda
- ¼ tsp salt
- ½ tsp ground nutmeg
- ½ tsp ground cinnamon
- ½ cup unsalted butter, softened
- 1 cup granulated sugar
- 2 large eggs
- 1 cup eggnog
- 1 tsp vanilla extract

For the Eggnog Frosting:

- ½ cup unsalted butter, softened
- 2 cups powdered sugar
- 2 tbsp eggnog
- 1 tsp vanilla extract
- ¼ tsp ground nutmeg (optional, for garnish)

Instructions

1. Preheat the Oven:

- Preheat your oven to 350°F (175°C). Line a 12-cup muffin tin with paper liners.

2. Prepare the Cupcake Batter:

- In a medium bowl, whisk together the flour, baking powder, baking soda, salt, nutmeg, and cinnamon.
- In a large bowl, cream together the softened butter and granulated sugar until light and fluffy.
- Beat in the eggs, one at a time, ensuring each is fully incorporated before adding the next.
- Mix in the vanilla extract.
- Gradually add the dry ingredients to the butter mixture, alternating with the eggnog, beginning and ending with the dry ingredients. Mix until just combined.

3. Bake the Cupcakes:

- Divide the batter evenly among the cupcake liners, filling each about 2/3 full.
- Bake for 18-22 minutes, or until a toothpick inserted into the center comes out clean.
- Allow the cupcakes to cool in the tin for 5 minutes before transferring them to a wire rack to cool completely.

4. Prepare the Eggnog Frosting:

- In a medium bowl, beat the softened butter until creamy.
- Gradually add the powdered sugar, beating well after each addition.
- Mix in the eggnog and vanilla extract until smooth and fluffy. If the frosting is too thick, add a little more eggnog; if too thin, add more powdered sugar.

5. Frost the Cupcakes:

- Once the cupcakes are completely cooled, frost them with the eggnog frosting.
- Garnish with a sprinkle of ground nutmeg if desired.

Enjoy these eggnog cupcakes with a cup of coffee or hot cocoa for a festive holiday treat! They're perfect for parties, family gatherings, or just a special dessert to enjoy during the holiday season.

Cinnamon Sugar Donuts

Ingredients

For the Donuts:

- 2 ½ cups all-purpose flour
- 1 cup granulated sugar
- 1 tbsp baking powder
- ½ tsp salt
- 1 tsp ground cinnamon
- ½ tsp ground nutmeg
- ½ cup whole milk
- 2 large eggs
- ¼ cup unsalted butter, melted
- 1 tsp vanilla extract

For the Cinnamon Sugar Coating:

- ¼ cup granulated sugar
- 1 tbsp ground cinnamon

Instructions

1. Preheat the Oven:

- Preheat your oven to 375°F (190°C). Grease a donut pan or lightly spray it with non-stick cooking spray.

2. Prepare the Donut Batter:

- In a large bowl, whisk together the flour, sugar, baking powder, salt, cinnamon, and nutmeg.
- In another bowl, mix together the milk, eggs, melted butter, and vanilla extract.
- Pour the wet ingredients into the dry ingredients and stir until just combined. Be careful not to overmix.

3. Fill the Donut Pan:

- Spoon or pipe the batter into the donut pan, filling each cavity about 2/3 full. If using a piping bag, cut off the tip to make it easier to fill the pan.

4. Bake the Donuts:

- Bake for 10-12 minutes, or until a toothpick inserted into the center comes out clean and the donuts are lightly golden.

- Allow the donuts to cool in the pan for 5 minutes before transferring them to a wire rack to cool completely.

5. Prepare the Cinnamon Sugar Coating:

- In a small bowl, mix together the granulated sugar and ground cinnamon.

6. Coat the Donuts:

- While the donuts are still slightly warm, brush them with a little melted butter (if desired) or dip them into the cinnamon sugar mixture to coat.

7. Serve:

- Enjoy the donuts fresh, while they're still warm, or store them in an airtight container for up to 3 days.

These cinnamon sugar donuts are perfect for breakfast or as a sweet treat any time of day. They're simple to make and incredibly satisfying with their warm, spicy flavor and sugary coating.

Rum Balls

Ingredients

- 2 cups (200g) finely crushed vanilla wafers or graham crackers
- 1 cup (100g) finely chopped nuts (e.g., walnuts, pecans, or almonds)
- 1 cup (120g) powdered sugar
- ¼ cup (25g) unsweetened cocoa powder
- ¼ cup (60ml) dark rum
- 2 tbsp light corn syrup or honey (for binding)
- 1 tsp vanilla extract (optional)

For Coating:

- ½ cup (50g) powdered sugar
- ¼ cup (25g) unsweetened cocoa powder
- Or just powdered sugar, cocoa powder, or finely chopped nuts (whichever you prefer)

Instructions

1. Prepare the Ingredients:

- In a large bowl, combine the crushed vanilla wafers or graham crackers, chopped nuts, powdered sugar, and cocoa powder.

2. Mix the Wet Ingredients:

- In a small bowl, mix the rum, corn syrup (or honey), and vanilla extract (if using) until well combined.

3. Combine Everything:

- Gradually add the wet ingredients to the dry mixture, stirring until the mixture is evenly combined and holds together when pressed. If the mixture is too dry, add a bit more rum or corn syrup. If it's too wet, add a bit more crushed cookies or nuts.

4. Form the Balls:

- Using your hands or a small cookie scoop, roll the mixture into 1-inch (2.5 cm) balls. Place them on a baking sheet lined with parchment paper or a silicone baking mat.

5. Coat the Rum Balls:

- In a small bowl, mix together the powdered sugar and cocoa powder (if using).
- Roll each rum ball in the mixture until evenly coated. You can also use just powdered sugar or cocoa powder, or roll in finely chopped nuts if you prefer.

6. Chill:

- Refrigerate the rum balls for at least 1 hour to let them set and the flavors meld together.

7. Serve:

- Enjoy your rum balls chilled or at room temperature. They can be stored in an airtight container in the refrigerator for up to 2 weeks.

Rum balls are rich and flavorful with a delightful texture, making them a perfect treat for special occasions or as a delightful gift for friends and family.

Holiday Fruitcake

Ingredients

For the Fruit and Nut Mix:

- 1 cup (150g) mixed dried fruit (such as raisins, currants, and chopped dried apricots)
- 1 cup (150g) chopped dates
- 1 cup (150g) chopped nuts (such as walnuts, pecans, or almonds)
- ½ cup (80g) candied fruit (such as cherries or citrus peel), chopped (optional)
- ¼ cup (60ml) orange juice or dark rum (for soaking)

For the Fruitcake:

- 1 ¼ cups (150g) all-purpose flour
- 1 tsp baking powder
- ½ tsp baking soda
- ¼ tsp salt
- 1 tsp ground cinnamon
- ½ tsp ground nutmeg
- ¼ tsp ground allspice
- ½ cup (115g) unsalted butter, softened
- ½ cup (100g) granulated sugar
- ¼ cup (50g) packed brown sugar
- 2 large eggs
- ¼ cup (60ml) honey
- ¼ cup (60ml) orange juice
- 1 tsp vanilla extract

For Soaking (Optional):

- Additional dark rum or brandy for brushing

Instructions

1. Prepare the Fruit and Nut Mix:

- In a medium bowl, combine the dried fruit, dates, nuts, and candied fruit (if using).
- Pour the orange juice or dark rum over the mixture and stir well to coat.
- Let the mixture soak for at least 1 hour or overnight for best results.

2. Preheat the Oven:

- Preheat your oven to 325°F (163°C). Grease and line a 9x5-inch (23x13 cm) loaf pan with parchment paper.

3. Prepare the Fruitcake Batter:

- In a medium bowl, whisk together the flour, baking powder, baking soda, salt, cinnamon, nutmeg, and allspice.
- In a large bowl, cream together the softened butter, granulated sugar, and brown sugar until light and fluffy.
- Beat in the eggs one at a time until fully incorporated.
- Mix in the honey, orange juice, and vanilla extract.
- Gradually add the dry ingredients to the wet mixture, stirring until just combined.

4. Fold in the Fruit and Nut Mixture:

- Gently fold the soaked fruit and nut mixture into the batter until evenly distributed.

5. Bake the Fruitcake:

- Pour the batter into the prepared loaf pan and smooth the top.
- Bake for 60-70 minutes, or until a toothpick inserted into the center comes out clean and the cake is golden brown.
- Let the fruitcake cool in the pan for 10 minutes, then transfer it to a wire rack to cool completely.

6. Optional: Soak with Alcohol:

- Once the cake is completely cooled, you can brush it with additional dark rum or brandy to enhance the flavor and keep it moist.
- Wrap the fruitcake in plastic wrap and store it in an airtight container. It can be kept at room temperature for up to 2 weeks or refrigerated for up to 1 month.

7. Serve:

- Slice the fruitcake and serve it as is, or with a dollop of cream cheese or a sprinkle of powdered sugar.

Enjoy this festive fruitcake as a delicious and traditional holiday treat! It's a rich, flavorful cake that improves with time, making it perfect for making ahead of the holidays.

Almond Biscotti

Ingredients

- 2 cups (240g) all-purpose flour
- 1 cup (200g) granulated sugar
- 1 tsp baking powder
- ¼ tsp salt
- ½ cup (115g) unsalted butter, softened
- 2 large eggs
- 1 tsp vanilla extract
- 1 tsp almond extract
- 1 cup (120g) whole almonds, toasted (or slivered almonds)
- 1 egg white (for brushing, optional)
- Coarse sugar (for sprinkling, optional)

Instructions

1. Preheat the Oven:

- Preheat your oven to 350°F (175°C). Line a baking sheet with parchment paper or a silicone baking mat.

2. Prepare the Dough:

- In a medium bowl, whisk together the flour, sugar, baking powder, and salt.
- In a large bowl, cream together the softened butter until light and fluffy.
- Beat in the eggs one at a time, then mix in the vanilla extract and almond extract.
- Gradually add the dry ingredients to the wet ingredients, mixing until just combined.
- Fold in the toasted almonds.

3. Shape the Dough:

- Divide the dough in half and shape each portion into a log about 12 inches long and 2 inches wide on the prepared baking sheet.
- Flatten the logs slightly with your hands or a spatula.

4. Bake the Logs:

- Bake in the preheated oven for 25-30 minutes, or until the logs are golden brown and firm to the touch.
- Allow the logs to cool on the baking sheet for about 10 minutes. This makes them easier to cut.

5. Slice and Second Bake:

- Transfer the logs to a cutting board and slice them diagonally into ½-inch to ¾-inch wide pieces.
- Arrange the slices cut-side up on the baking sheet.
- Return the biscotti to the oven and bake for an additional 10-15 minutes, or until they are crisp and golden brown. You may need to flip the biscotti halfway through baking to ensure they are evenly toasted.

6. Cool and Store:

- Allow the biscotti to cool completely on a wire rack.
- Store the cooled biscotti in an airtight container for up to 2 weeks. They can also be frozen for up to 3 months.

7. Optional Glaze:

- For a touch of sweetness, you can drizzle the cooled biscotti with a simple glaze made from powdered sugar and a bit of milk or lemon juice.

Enjoy your homemade almond biscotti with a cup of coffee, tea, or hot chocolate. They're perfect for dipping and have a satisfying crunch that's hard to resist!

Chocolate Hazelnut Truffles

Ingredients

- 1 cup (240ml) heavy cream
- 8 oz (225g) semi-sweet chocolate, coarsely chopped
- ¼ cup (60ml) hazelnut liqueur (e.g., Frangelico) or 2 tsp hazelnut extract
- ½ cup (50g) finely chopped toasted hazelnuts
- Cocoa powder, chopped hazelnuts, or melted chocolate (for coating)

Instructions

1. Prepare the Ganache:

- In a small saucepan, heat the heavy cream over medium heat until it just begins to simmer. Do not let it boil.
- Remove the saucepan from heat and add the chopped chocolate. Let it sit for about 1-2 minutes to allow the chocolate to melt.
- Stir the mixture until smooth and completely combined.
- Mix in the hazelnut liqueur or hazelnut extract.

2. Chill the Ganache:

- Let the ganache cool to room temperature, then cover it with plastic wrap and refrigerate for at least 2 hours, or until it is firm enough to scoop.

3. Shape the Truffles:

- Once the ganache is firm, use a small cookie scoop or a teaspoon to scoop out portions of the ganache and roll them into balls between your hands.
- Roll each truffle in finely chopped toasted hazelnuts, cocoa powder, or melted chocolate to coat. If using melted chocolate for coating, let the coated truffles set on a parchment-lined baking sheet until the chocolate is firm.

4. Chill and Store:

- Transfer the finished truffles to a parchment-lined tray or an airtight container. Refrigerate until ready to serve.
- Truffles can be stored in the refrigerator for up to 2 weeks or in the freezer for up to 2 months.

5. Optional Decoration:

- For added flair, drizzle some melted chocolate over the coated truffles or sprinkle a pinch of sea salt on top before the coating sets.

These chocolate hazelnut truffles are smooth, creamy, and packed with rich flavor. They're perfect for holiday parties, special occasions, or simply as a delightful treat to enjoy anytime!

Gingerbread Cake

Ingredients

For the Cake:

- 2 ½ cups (310g) all-purpose flour
- 1 ½ tsp baking powder
- 1 ½ tsp baking soda
- ¼ tsp salt
- 1 ½ tsp ground ginger
- 1 ½ tsp ground cinnamon
- ½ tsp ground cloves
- ¼ tsp ground nutmeg
- ¾ cup (170g) unsalted butter, softened
- 1 cup (200g) granulated sugar
- 1 cup (240ml) molasses
- 2 large eggs
- 1 cup (240ml) hot water

For the Cream Cheese Frosting (Optional):

- 8 oz (225g) cream cheese, softened
- ¼ cup (60g) unsalted butter, softened
- 2 cups (240g) powdered sugar
- 1 tsp vanilla extract

Instructions

1. Preheat the Oven:

- Preheat your oven to 350°F (175°C). Grease and flour a 9x13-inch (23x33 cm) baking pan or two 9-inch round cake pans.

2. Prepare the Dry Ingredients:

- In a medium bowl, whisk together the flour, baking powder, baking soda, salt, ginger, cinnamon, cloves, and nutmeg.

3. Cream the Butter and Sugar:

- In a large bowl, beat the softened butter and granulated sugar together until light and fluffy.

4. Add Molasses and Eggs:

- Mix in the molasses until well combined.

- Beat in the eggs, one at a time, until fully incorporated.

5. Combine Wet and Dry Ingredients:

- Gradually add the dry ingredients to the butter mixture, alternating with the hot water. Begin and end with the dry ingredients, mixing just until combined. The batter will be quite thin, but that's normal.

6. Bake the Cake:

- Pour the batter into the prepared baking pan(s) and smooth the top.
- Bake for 30-35 minutes (for a 9x13-inch pan) or 25-30 minutes (for 9-inch round pans), or until a toothpick inserted into the center comes out clean.
- Allow the cake to cool in the pan for 10 minutes before transferring it to a wire rack to cool completely.

7. Prepare the Cream Cheese Frosting (Optional):

- In a medium bowl, beat the softened cream cheese and butter together until smooth and creamy.
- Gradually add the powdered sugar, beating until the frosting is light and fluffy.
- Mix in the vanilla extract.

8. Frost and Serve:

- Once the cake is completely cooled, frost with the cream cheese frosting if using.
- Garnish with additional spices or a sprinkle of powdered sugar if desired.

9. Store:

- Store the frosted or unfrosted cake in an airtight container at room temperature for up to 3 days, or in the refrigerator for up to a week.

Enjoy your gingerbread cake with a cup of tea or coffee, or as a festive dessert during the holiday season. It's a wonderful blend of warm spices and sweet molasses that's sure to be a hit!

Caramel Apple Cookies

Ingredients

- 1 cup (230g) unsalted butter, softened
- ¾ cup (150g) granulated sugar
- ¾ cup (165g) packed brown sugar
- 2 large eggs
- 1 tsp vanilla extract
- 2 ¼ cups (280g) all-purpose flour
- 1 tsp baking soda
- ½ tsp baking powder
- ½ tsp salt
- 1 tsp ground cinnamon
- 1 cup (100g) finely chopped apples (peeled and cored)
- 1 cup (150g) caramel bits or chopped caramel candies
- 1 cup (100g) chopped pecans or walnuts (optional)

Instructions

1. Preheat the Oven:

- Preheat your oven to 350°F (175°C). Line baking sheets with parchment paper or silicone baking mats.

2. Prepare the Dry Ingredients:

- In a medium bowl, whisk together the flour, baking soda, baking powder, salt, and ground cinnamon. Set aside.

3. Cream the Butter and Sugars:

- In a large bowl, beat the softened butter, granulated sugar, and brown sugar together until light and fluffy.

4. Add Eggs and Vanilla:

- Beat in the eggs, one at a time, mixing well after each addition.
- Mix in the vanilla extract.

5. Combine Wet and Dry Ingredients:

- Gradually add the dry ingredients to the butter mixture, mixing just until combined.

6. Fold in Apples and Caramel:

- Gently fold in the finely chopped apples, caramel bits, and chopped nuts (if using) until evenly distributed.

7. Scoop the Dough:

- Using a cookie scoop or tablespoon, drop rounded balls of dough onto the prepared baking sheets, spacing them about 2 inches apart.

8. Bake the Cookies:

- Bake for 10-12 minutes, or until the edges are golden brown but the centers are still soft.
- Allow the cookies to cool on the baking sheets for a few minutes before transferring them to a wire rack to cool completely.

9. Optional: Drizzle with Caramel:

- For extra indulgence, you can drizzle melted caramel over the cooled cookies.

10. Store:

- Store the cookies in an airtight container at room temperature for up to 1 week. They can also be frozen for up to 3 months.

Enjoy your caramel apple cookies with a cup of tea or coffee, or as a sweet treat any time of day. The combination of tender apples, sweet caramel, and warm spices makes these cookies irresistible!

Mincemeat Pies

Ingredients

For the Mincemeat Filling:

- 2 cups (300g) mixed dried fruit (such as raisins, currants, and sultanas)
- 1 cup (150g) chopped dried apricots
- ½ cup (70g) finely chopped apples (peeled and cored)
- ½ cup (75g) chopped nuts (such as almonds or walnuts)
- ¼ cup (60ml) brandy or orange juice
- ¼ cup (50g) dark brown sugar
- 1 tsp ground cinnamon
- ½ tsp ground nutmeg
- ¼ tsp ground cloves
- 2 tbsp lemon juice
- 1 tbsp grated lemon zest
- 1 tbsp grated orange zest

For the Pastry:

- 2 ½ cups (320g) all-purpose flour
- ½ cup (100g) granulated sugar
- 1 tsp salt
- 1 cup (230g) unsalted butter, cold and cut into cubes
- 1 large egg
- 2-4 tbsp cold water

For Assembly:

- 1 egg, beaten (for egg wash)
- Granulated sugar (for sprinkling, optional)

Instructions

1. Prepare the Mincemeat Filling:

- In a large bowl, combine the mixed dried fruit, chopped dried apricots, finely chopped apples, and chopped nuts.
- Stir in the brandy or orange juice, dark brown sugar, ground cinnamon, ground nutmeg, ground cloves, lemon juice, lemon zest, and orange zest.
- Mix well and let the mixture sit for at least 1 hour, or overnight for the flavors to meld. If making ahead, store in an airtight container in the refrigerator for up to 2 weeks.

2. Prepare the Pastry:

- In a large bowl, whisk together the flour, granulated sugar, and salt.
- Cut in the cold butter using a pastry cutter or your fingers until the mixture resembles coarse crumbs with pea-sized pieces of butter.
- Beat the egg and add it to the flour mixture. Mix until combined.
- Gradually add cold water, one tablespoon at a time, until the dough just comes together.
- Divide the dough in half, form each half into a disk, wrap in plastic wrap, and refrigerate for at least 30 minutes.

3. Preheat the Oven:

- Preheat your oven to 375°F (190°C). Grease a 12-cup muffin tin or individual tart pans.

4. Roll Out the Dough:

- On a lightly floured surface, roll out one disk of dough to about ⅛ inch (3 mm) thickness.
- Cut out circles of dough slightly larger than the muffin tin cups or tart pans (about 4 inches/10 cm for standard muffin tins).

5. Assemble the Pies:

- Press the dough circles into the muffin tin cups or tart pans, gently molding them to fit.
- Spoon a generous amount of mincemeat filling into each pastry shell.

6. Top the Pies:

- Roll out the second disk of dough and cut it into smaller circles or shapes to fit on top of the filled pies.
- Place the tops on the filled pies and press the edges to seal. Cut small slits in the tops to allow steam to escape.
- Brush the tops with the beaten egg and sprinkle with granulated sugar if desired.

7. Bake the Pies:

- Bake for 20-25 minutes, or until the pastry is golden brown and the filling is bubbling.
- Allow the pies to cool in the tin for 5 minutes before transferring them to a wire rack to cool completely.

8. Serve and Store:

- Serve warm or at room temperature. Mincemeat pies can be stored in an airtight container at room temperature for up to 1 week. They can also be frozen for up to 3 months.

Enjoy your mincemeat pies with a dusting of powdered sugar or a dollop of whipped cream. They're a wonderfully festive treat that's sure to be a hit during the holiday season!

Snowball Cookies

Ingredients

- 1 cup (230g) unsalted butter, softened
- ½ cup (60g) powdered sugar, plus extra for coating
- 1 tsp vanilla extract
- 2 ¼ cups (280g) all-purpose flour
- ¼ tsp salt
- 1 cup (100g) finely chopped nuts (such as walnuts, pecans, or almonds)

Instructions

1. Preheat the Oven:

- Preheat your oven to 350°F (175°C). Line a baking sheet with parchment paper or a silicone baking mat.

2. Cream the Butter and Sugar:

- In a large bowl, beat the softened butter and ½ cup powdered sugar together until light and fluffy.

3. Add Vanilla Extract:

- Mix in the vanilla extract until well combined.

4. Combine Dry Ingredients:

- In a separate bowl, whisk together the flour and salt.
- Gradually add the dry ingredients to the butter mixture, mixing until just combined.

5. Fold in Nuts:

- Gently fold in the finely chopped nuts.

6. Shape the Cookies:

- Roll the dough into 1-inch (2.5 cm) balls and place them on the prepared baking sheet, spacing them about 1 inch (2.5 cm) apart.

7. Bake the Cookies:

- Bake for 12-15 minutes, or until the cookies are set and just starting to turn golden on the bottoms.
- Remove from the oven and let cool on the baking sheet for a few minutes.

8. Coat in Powdered Sugar:

- While the cookies are still warm but not hot, roll them in powdered sugar to coat.
- Transfer the cookies to a wire rack to cool completely. Once cooled, roll them in powdered sugar again for an extra snowy coating.

9. Store:

- Store the cooled cookies in an airtight container at room temperature for up to 1 week. They can also be frozen for up to 3 months.

Tips:

- **Chill the Dough:** If the dough is too soft to handle, you can chill it in the refrigerator for about 30 minutes to make it easier to roll into balls.
- **Make Ahead:** These cookies are great for making ahead of time and freeze well. Just be sure to coat them in powdered sugar after thawing.

These snowball cookies are buttery, tender, and melt-in-your-mouth delicious. They make a beautiful addition to any cookie platter and are sure to be a hit at your next holiday gathering!

Chocolate Caramel Tart

Ingredients

For the Tart Crust:

- 1 ¼ cups (160g) all-purpose flour
- ¼ cup (30g) granulated sugar
- ¼ tsp salt
- ½ cup (115g) unsalted butter, cold and cut into small pieces
- 1 large egg yolk
- 2-3 tbsp ice water

For the Caramel Filling:

- 1 cup (200g) granulated sugar
- 6 tbsp (85g) unsalted butter, cut into pieces
- ½ cup (120ml) heavy cream
- ¼ tsp salt

For the Chocolate Ganache:

- 8 oz (225g) semi-sweet or dark chocolate, finely chopped
- 1 cup (240ml) heavy cream
- 1 tbsp unsalted butter
- 1 tsp vanilla extract (optional)

For Garnish (Optional):

- Sea salt flakes
- Chopped nuts (e.g., toasted pecans or almonds)

Instructions

1. Prepare the Tart Crust:

- In a medium bowl, whisk together the flour, sugar, and salt.
- Add the cold butter and use a pastry cutter or your fingers to work it into the flour mixture until it resembles coarse crumbs.
- In a small bowl, whisk the egg yolk and add it to the flour mixture. Mix until combined.
- Gradually add ice water, one tablespoon at a time, until the dough just comes together.
- Form the dough into a disk, wrap in plastic wrap, and refrigerate for at least 30 minutes.

2. Preheat the Oven:

- Preheat your oven to 350°F (175°C).

3. Roll and Bake the Tart Crust:

- On a lightly floured surface, roll out the dough to about ¼ inch (6 mm) thick.
- Carefully transfer the dough to a 9-inch (23 cm) tart pan with a removable bottom. Press the dough into the edges and trim any excess.
- Refrigerate the crust for another 10-15 minutes.
- Line the crust with parchment paper and fill with pie weights or dried beans.
- Bake for 15 minutes. Remove the parchment and weights, then bake for an additional 5-10 minutes until the crust is golden brown.
- Allow the crust to cool completely on a wire rack.

4. Prepare the Caramel Filling:

- In a medium saucepan over medium heat, cook the granulated sugar until it melts and turns a deep amber color, swirling the pan occasionally.
- Remove from heat and carefully add the butter, stirring until melted and combined.
- Gradually pour in the heavy cream while continuing to stir. Be cautious, as the mixture will bubble up.
- Stir in the salt and let the caramel cool for a few minutes.
- Pour the caramel into the cooled tart crust and spread it evenly. Refrigerate for at least 1 hour to set.

5. Prepare the Chocolate Ganache:

- Place the chopped chocolate in a heatproof bowl.
- In a small saucepan, heat the heavy cream until it just begins to simmer. Pour the cream over the chopped chocolate.
- Let sit for 2-3 minutes, then stir until smooth and glossy.
- Stir in the butter and vanilla extract, if using.

6. Assemble the Tart:

- Pour the chocolate ganache over the set caramel layer, spreading it evenly.
- Refrigerate the tart for at least 2 hours, or until the ganache is set.

7. Garnish (Optional):

- Before serving, you can sprinkle the tart with sea salt flakes or garnish with chopped nuts for added texture and flavor.

8. Serve:

- Remove the tart from the pan and transfer it to a serving platter.
- Slice and enjoy!

This chocolate caramel tart is a rich and elegant dessert that combines layers of smooth caramel and velvety chocolate, all encased in a buttery tart crust. It's sure to impress your guests and satisfy your sweet tooth!

Buttery Shortbread

Ingredients

- 1 cup (230g) unsalted butter, softened
- ½ cup (100g) granulated sugar
- ¼ cup (50g) packed brown sugar (optional for a hint of caramel flavor)
- 2 cups (240g) all-purpose flour
- ¼ tsp salt
- 1 tsp vanilla extract (optional)
- ¼ cup (30g) cornstarch (optional, for extra crumbly texture)

Instructions

1. Preheat the Oven:

- Preheat your oven to 325°F (165°C). Line a baking sheet with parchment paper or a silicone baking mat.

2. Cream the Butter and Sugar:

- In a large bowl, beat the softened butter and granulated sugar together until light and fluffy.
- If using, mix in the brown sugar for added depth of flavor.

3. Add Vanilla (Optional):

- If using vanilla extract, mix it in at this stage.

4. Combine Dry Ingredients:

- In a separate bowl, whisk together the flour, salt, and cornstarch (if using).

5. Mix Dry and Wet Ingredients:

- Gradually add the dry ingredients to the butter mixture, mixing until just combined. The dough will be somewhat crumbly but should hold together when pressed.

6. Shape the Dough:

- Turn the dough out onto a lightly floured surface and gently press it into a flat disk. You can roll it out to about ½ inch (1.2 cm) thickness and cut into shapes with cookie cutters, or you can press it directly into a baking pan for a more rustic look.
- If rolling out, transfer the cut cookies to the prepared baking sheet.
- If pressing into a pan, press the dough evenly into the bottom of an 8-inch (20 cm) square pan or a 9-inch (23 cm) round tart pan. Score the surface with a knife to create squares or wedges for easier cutting after baking.

7. Bake the Shortbread:

- Bake in the preheated oven for 15-20 minutes, or until the edges are lightly golden. The shortbread should be firm to the touch and not overly browned.
- If using a pan, let the shortbread cool in the pan for about 10 minutes before cutting along the scored lines. Then, transfer to a wire rack to cool completely.

8. Store:

- Once cooled, store the shortbread in an airtight container at room temperature for up to 1 week. It can also be frozen for up to 3 months.

9. Optional: Decorate:

- For a festive touch, you can sprinkle the shortbread with a bit of granulated sugar before baking or dip the cooled cookies in chocolate for extra indulgence.

Buttery shortbread is a timeless treat that pairs wonderfully with a cup of tea or coffee. Its simple ingredients and delightful texture make it a favorite for both casual snacking and elegant occasions. Enjoy your homemade shortbread!

Red Velvet Cake

Ingredients

For the Cake:

- 2 ½ cups (320g) all-purpose flour
- 1 ½ cups (300g) granulated sugar
- 1 tsp baking powder
- 1 tsp baking soda
- ½ tsp salt
- 1 tsp cocoa powder
- 1 cup (240ml) vegetable oil
- 1 cup (240ml) buttermilk, room temperature
- 2 large eggs
- 2 tbsp (30ml) red food coloring (preferably gel or paste for a vibrant color)
- 1 tsp vanilla extract
- 1 tsp white vinegar

For the Cream Cheese Frosting:

- 8 oz (225g) cream cheese, softened
- ½ cup (115g) unsalted butter, softened
- 4 cups (480g) powdered sugar
- 1 tsp vanilla extract

Instructions

1. Preheat the Oven:

- Preheat your oven to 350°F (175°C). Grease and flour two 9-inch (23 cm) round cake pans, or line them with parchment paper.

2. Prepare the Dry Ingredients:

- In a medium bowl, whisk together the flour, granulated sugar, baking powder, baking soda, salt, and cocoa powder. Set aside.

3. Mix the Wet Ingredients:

- In a large bowl, whisk together the vegetable oil and buttermilk until well combined.
- Beat in the eggs, one at a time, mixing well after each addition.
- Stir in the red food coloring, vanilla extract, and white vinegar.

4. Combine Wet and Dry Ingredients:

- Gradually add the dry ingredients to the wet ingredients, mixing just until combined. Be careful not to overmix.

5. Bake the Cake:

- Divide the batter evenly between the prepared cake pans.
- Bake for 25-30 minutes, or until a toothpick inserted into the center of the cakes comes out clean.
- Allow the cakes to cool in the pans for about 10 minutes, then transfer them to a wire rack to cool completely.

6. Prepare the Cream Cheese Frosting:

- In a large bowl, beat the softened cream cheese and butter together until smooth and creamy.
- Gradually add the powdered sugar, beating until fully combined and the frosting is light and fluffy.
- Mix in the vanilla extract.

7. Frost the Cake:

- Once the cakes are completely cooled, spread a layer of cream cheese frosting on top of one of the cake layers.
- Place the second cake layer on top and frost the top and sides of the cake.
- Decorate as desired. You can use a piping bag to create decorative swirls or add sprinkles for a festive touch.

8. Serve and Store:

- Serve the cake at room temperature. Store any leftovers in an airtight container in the refrigerator for up to 5 days. The cake can also be frozen for up to 3 months.

Enjoy your homemade red velvet cake with its rich flavor and beautiful color! It's a perfect choice for celebrations, special occasions, or simply as a treat for yourself.

Mint Chocolate Brownies

Ingredients

For the Brownies:

- 1 cup (230g) unsalted butter
- 2 cups (400g) granulated sugar
- 1 cup (90g) unsweetened cocoa powder
- ½ tsp salt
- 1 tsp vanilla extract
- 4 large eggs
- 1 cup (125g) all-purpose flour
- 1 cup (150g) chocolate chips or chunks (optional)

For the Mint Layer:

- 1 cup (240ml) heavy cream
- 1 cup (175g) semi-sweet chocolate chips
- 2 tbsp unsalted butter
- 1-2 tsp peppermint extract (adjust to taste)
- Green food coloring (optional)

For the Chocolate Ganache:

- 1 cup (175g) semi-sweet chocolate chips
- ½ cup (120ml) heavy cream

Instructions

1. Preheat the Oven:

- Preheat your oven to 350°F (175°C). Line a 9x13-inch (23x33 cm) baking pan with parchment paper or foil, leaving some overhang for easy removal.

2. Prepare the Brownie Batter:

- In a medium saucepan, melt the butter over low heat. Remove from heat and stir in the granulated sugar, cocoa powder, and salt.
- Beat in the vanilla extract and then the eggs, one at a time, mixing well after each addition.
- Stir in the flour until just combined. If using, fold in the chocolate chips or chunks.

3. Bake the Brownies:

- Pour the brownie batter into the prepared pan and spread it evenly.

- Bake for 25-30 minutes, or until a toothpick inserted into the center comes out with a few moist crumbs. The brownies should be set but still fudgy.
- Allow the brownies to cool completely in the pan on a wire rack before adding the mint layer.

4. Prepare the Mint Layer:

- Heat the heavy cream in a small saucepan over medium heat until it just begins to simmer.
- Pour the hot cream over the chocolate chips in a heatproof bowl. Let it sit for 1-2 minutes, then stir until smooth.
- Mix in the butter until melted and fully incorporated.
- Stir in the peppermint extract. Add a few drops of green food coloring if desired to achieve a minty green color.
- Spread the mint mixture evenly over the cooled brownies. Refrigerate for about 30 minutes, or until the mint layer is set.

5. Prepare the Chocolate Ganache:

- In a small saucepan, heat the heavy cream over medium heat until it just begins to simmer.
- Pour the hot cream over the chocolate chips in a heatproof bowl. Let it sit for 1-2 minutes, then stir until smooth and glossy.

6. Assemble the Brownies:

- Pour the chocolate ganache over the set mint layer, spreading it evenly.
- Refrigerate the brownies for at least 1 hour to allow the ganache to set before cutting.

7. Serve:

- Once the ganache is set, lift the brownies out of the pan using the parchment overhang. Cut into squares or bars.

8. Store:

- Store the brownies in an airtight container in the refrigerator for up to 1 week. They can also be frozen for up to 3 months.

These mint chocolate brownies are a decadent treat with layers of rich chocolate and refreshing mint. They're perfect for holiday gatherings, special occasions, or just a sweet indulgence. Enjoy!

Linzer Cookies

Ingredients

For the Dough:

- 1 cup (230g) unsalted butter, softened
- ½ cup (100g) granulated sugar
- ½ cup (60g) packed brown sugar
- 1 large egg
- 1 tsp vanilla extract
- 1 ¾ cups (220g) all-purpose flour
- 1 cup (100g) finely ground almonds or almond flour
- ¼ tsp salt
- ¼ tsp ground cinnamon (optional)

For the Filling:

- ¾ cup (240g) fruit jam or preserves (such as raspberry, apricot, or strawberry)

For Dusting:

- Powdered sugar

Instructions

1. Preheat the Oven:

- Preheat your oven to 350°F (175°C). Line two baking sheets with parchment paper or silicone baking mats.

2. Prepare the Dough:

- In a large bowl, cream together the softened butter, granulated sugar, and brown sugar until light and fluffy.
- Beat in the egg and vanilla extract until well combined.
- In a separate bowl, whisk together the flour, finely ground almonds (or almond flour), salt, and ground cinnamon (if using).
- Gradually add the dry ingredients to the butter mixture, mixing until just combined. The dough should be soft but not sticky.

3. Roll and Cut the Dough:

- Divide the dough in half and roll out each portion on a lightly floured surface to about ¼ inch (6 mm) thickness.
- Use a round cookie cutter to cut out cookies from one half of the dough. Use a smaller round cutter or a decorative cutter to cut out centers from the remaining cookies.

- Place the cut-out cookies on the prepared baking sheets.

4. Bake the Cookies:

- Bake in the preheated oven for 10-12 minutes, or until the edges are lightly golden.
- Allow the cookies to cool on the baking sheets for a few minutes before transferring them to a wire rack to cool completely.

5. Assemble the Cookies:

- Once the cookies are completely cooled, spread a small amount of fruit jam or preserves on the flat side of the whole cookies.
- Place the cookies with the cut-out centers on top of the jam-covered cookies, gently pressing them together.

6. Dust with Powdered Sugar:

- Lightly dust the tops of the cookies with powdered sugar.

7. Store:

- Store the assembled Linzer cookies in an airtight container at room temperature for up to 1 week. They can also be frozen for up to 3 months. If freezing, it's best to freeze the cookies without the jam and add it after thawing.

Linzer cookies are perfect for holiday baking, special occasions, or just as a delightful treat. The combination of buttery almond cookies with sweet fruit jam makes them irresistibly delicious!

Bourbon Pecan Pie

Ingredients

For the Pie Crust:

- 1 ¼ cups (160g) all-purpose flour
- ¼ cup (50g) granulated sugar
- ¼ tsp salt
- ½ cup (115g) unsalted butter, cold and cut into small pieces
- 1 large egg yolk
- 2-4 tbsp ice water

For the Filling:

- 1 cup (240ml) light corn syrup
- 1 cup (220g) packed light brown sugar
- ¼ cup (60ml) unsalted butter, melted
- 4 large eggs
- ¼ cup (60ml) bourbon
- 1 tsp vanilla extract
- 2 cups (200g) pecan halves
- A pinch of salt

Instructions

1. Prepare the Pie Crust:

- In a medium bowl, whisk together the flour, granulated sugar, and salt.
- Cut in the cold butter using a pastry cutter or your fingers until the mixture resembles coarse crumbs with pea-sized pieces of butter.
- In a small bowl, whisk the egg yolk and add it to the flour mixture. Mix until combined.
- Gradually add ice water, one tablespoon at a time, until the dough just comes together.
- Form the dough into a disk, wrap in plastic wrap, and refrigerate for at least 30 minutes.

2. Preheat the Oven:

- Preheat your oven to 350°F (175°C).

3. Roll Out the Dough:

- On a lightly floured surface, roll out the dough to about ⅛ inch (3 mm) thickness.
- Carefully transfer the dough to a 9-inch (23 cm) pie dish, gently pressing it into the edges. Trim any excess dough and crimp the edges if desired.
- Refrigerate the pie crust while you prepare the filling.

4. Toast the Pecans:

- Spread the pecan halves on a baking sheet and toast in the preheated oven for 6-8 minutes, or until fragrant. Allow them to cool before using.

5. Prepare the Filling:

- In a large bowl, whisk together the corn syrup, brown sugar, melted butter, eggs, bourbon, vanilla extract, and a pinch of salt until smooth and well combined.

6. Assemble the Pie:

- Arrange the toasted pecan halves evenly over the bottom of the chilled pie crust.
- Pour the filling mixture over the pecans, making sure they are evenly distributed.

7. Bake the Pie:

- Bake in the preheated oven for 50-60 minutes, or until the filling is set and the top is golden brown. The pie should still have a slight jiggle in the center when gently shaken.
- If the crust or the edges start to brown too quickly, cover them with aluminum foil to prevent burning.

8. Cool and Serve:

- Allow the pie to cool completely on a wire rack before serving. This will help the filling set properly.
- Serve the pie at room temperature or slightly warmed, with a dollop of whipped cream or a scoop of vanilla ice cream if desired.

9. Store:

- Store the pie in an airtight container at room temperature for up to 3 days. It can also be refrigerated for up to a week.

This bourbon pecan pie is a rich, flavorful dessert that adds a touch of sophistication to any occasion. The combination of sweet, nutty pecans with a hint of bourbon makes it a memorable treat for holiday gatherings or special celebrations. Enjoy!

Cranberry Almond Biscotti

Ingredients

- 1 ½ cups (190g) all-purpose flour
- ½ tsp baking powder
- ¼ tsp salt
- ¼ cup (50g) granulated sugar
- ¼ cup (50g) packed brown sugar
- ¼ cup (60ml) unsalted butter, melted and cooled
- 2 large eggs
- 1 tsp vanilla extract
- 1 tsp almond extract
- ½ cup (60g) dried cranberries
- ½ cup (60g) sliced almonds
- Optional: Zest of 1 orange (for extra flavor)

Instructions

1. Preheat the Oven:

- Preheat your oven to 350°F (175°C). Line a baking sheet with parchment paper.

2. Mix Dry Ingredients:

- In a medium bowl, whisk together the flour, baking powder, and salt.

3. Combine Wet Ingredients:

- In a large bowl, beat together the granulated sugar, brown sugar, melted butter, eggs, vanilla extract, and almond extract until smooth and well combined.

4. Combine Wet and Dry Ingredients:

- Gradually add the dry ingredients to the wet ingredients, mixing until just combined.
- Fold in the dried cranberries, sliced almonds, and orange zest if using.

5. Shape and Bake the Dough:

- Transfer the dough to the prepared baking sheet. With floured hands or a spatula, shape the dough into a log approximately 12 inches (30 cm) long and 3 inches (7.5 cm) wide.
- Bake for 25-30 minutes, or until the log is golden brown and firm to the touch.

6. Cool and Slice:

- Remove the log from the oven and let it cool on the baking sheet for about 10 minutes.

- Transfer the log to a cutting board and, using a serrated knife, slice it diagonally into ½-inch (1.25 cm) wide pieces.

7. Second Bake:

- Arrange the sliced biscotti, cut side down, on the baking sheet.
- Return to the oven and bake for an additional 10-15 minutes, or until the biscotti are crisp and golden brown.
- Allow the biscotti to cool completely on a wire rack.

8. Store:

- Store the cooled biscotti in an airtight container at room temperature for up to 2 weeks. They can also be frozen for up to 3 months.

Optional Glaze:

- For a touch of sweetness, you can drizzle the cooled biscotti with a simple glaze made from mixing powdered sugar with a small amount of milk or lemon juice.

These cranberry almond biscotti are perfect for enjoying with a hot beverage or for gifting during the holidays. Their crunchy texture and delightful flavors make them a treat that's sure to please!

Peppermint Hot Cocoa Cookies

Ingredients

For the Cookies:

- 1 ½ cups (190g) all-purpose flour
- ¼ cup (20g) unsweetened cocoa powder
- 1 tsp baking powder
- ½ tsp baking soda
- ¼ tsp salt
- ½ cup (115g) unsalted butter, softened
- ½ cup (100g) granulated sugar
- ½ cup (100g) packed brown sugar
- 1 large egg
- 1 tsp vanilla extract
- ½ cup (120ml) milk (whole or 2%)
- ½ cup (80g) mini marshmallows
- ¼ cup (30g) crushed peppermint candies or candy canes (for mix-in and garnish)

For the Peppermint Frosting:

- 1 cup (230g) unsalted butter, softened
- 3-4 cups (360-480g) powdered sugar
- 2-3 tbsp heavy cream (or milk)
- 1 tsp vanilla extract
- ¼ tsp peppermint extract (adjust to taste)
- A few drops of red food coloring (optional)

Instructions

1. Preheat the Oven:

- Preheat your oven to 350°F (175°C). Line two baking sheets with parchment paper or silicone baking mats.

2. Prepare the Cookie Dough:

- In a medium bowl, whisk together the flour, cocoa powder, baking powder, baking soda, and salt.
- In a large bowl, cream together the softened butter, granulated sugar, and brown sugar until light and fluffy.
- Beat in the egg and vanilla extract until well combined.
- Gradually add the dry ingredients to the wet ingredients, mixing until just combined.
- Stir in the milk until the dough is smooth.
- Fold in the mini marshmallows and crushed peppermint candies.

3. Scoop and Bake:

- Using a cookie scoop or tablespoon, drop rounded balls of dough onto the prepared baking sheets, spacing them about 2 inches apart.
- Bake for 10-12 minutes, or until the edges are set and the centers are slightly soft. The cookies will firm up as they cool.
- Allow the cookies to cool on the baking sheets for about 5 minutes, then transfer to a wire rack to cool completely.

4. Prepare the Peppermint Frosting:

- In a large bowl, beat the softened butter until creamy.
- Gradually add the powdered sugar, one cup at a time, beating well after each addition.
- Add 2 tablespoons of heavy cream (or milk), vanilla extract, and peppermint extract. Beat until smooth and fluffy. Add more cream if needed to achieve the desired consistency.
- If desired, add a few drops of red food coloring and mix until well combined.

5. Frost the Cookies:

- Once the cookies are completely cooled, spread a dollop of peppermint frosting on top of each cookie.
- Garnish with additional crushed peppermint candies if desired.

6. Store:

- Store the frosted cookies in an airtight container at room temperature for up to 1 week. The cookies can also be frozen without frosting for up to 3 months. Frost after thawing if desired.

These peppermint hot cocoa cookies are perfect for holiday gatherings, cozy winter evenings, or as a delightful treat for yourself. Enjoy their rich chocolate flavor with a festive peppermint twist!

White Chocolate Cranberry Bark

Ingredients

- 12 oz (340g) white chocolate, chopped (or white chocolate chips)
- 1 cup (120g) dried cranberries
- ½ cup (60g) chopped nuts (such as pistachios, almonds, or walnuts)
- ¼ cup (30g) mini pretzels or crushed graham crackers (optional, for added crunch)
- ¼ tsp sea salt (optional, for sprinkling)

Instructions

1. Prepare Your Workspace:

- Line a baking sheet with parchment paper or a silicone baking mat.

2. Melt the White Chocolate:

- In a heatproof bowl, melt the white chocolate over a double boiler (a bowl set over a pot of simmering water), stirring occasionally until smooth. Alternatively, you can melt the chocolate in the microwave in 20-30 second intervals, stirring after each interval until fully melted and smooth.

3. Mix in the Add-Ins:

- Once the white chocolate is melted, remove it from the heat. Stir in the dried cranberries and chopped nuts (and mini pretzels or graham crackers if using).

4. Spread the Mixture:

- Pour the white chocolate mixture onto the prepared baking sheet. Use a spatula to spread it into an even layer about ¼ inch (6 mm) thick.

5. Add Final Touches:

- Sprinkle a pinch of sea salt over the top if desired, for a touch of contrast.

6. Chill and Set:

- Refrigerate the bark for at least 1-2 hours, or until it is completely set and firm.

7. Break into Pieces:

- Once set, remove the bark from the parchment paper and break it into irregular pieces.

8. Store:

- Store the white chocolate cranberry bark in an airtight container in the refrigerator for up to 2 weeks. It can also be kept at room temperature for up to 1 week, depending on the climate.

9. Optional Decorating:

- For an extra festive touch, you can drizzle additional melted white chocolate over the top or sprinkle extra cranberries and nuts before chilling.

This white chocolate cranberry bark is a wonderfully easy and elegant treat that's sure to be a hit at any holiday gathering. Enjoy!

Sweet Potato Pie

Ingredients

For the Pie Crust:

- 1 ¼ cups (160g) all-purpose flour
- ¼ cup (50g) granulated sugar
- ¼ tsp salt
- ½ cup (115g) unsalted butter, cold and cut into small pieces
- 1 large egg yolk
- 2-4 tbsp ice water

For the Sweet Potato Filling:

- 2 cups (450g) cooked sweet potato (about 2 medium sweet potatoes)
- ¾ cup (150g) granulated sugar
- ¼ cup (50g) packed brown sugar
- 1 tsp ground cinnamon
- ¼ tsp ground nutmeg
- ¼ tsp ground ginger
- ¼ tsp salt
- 3 large eggs
- 1 cup (240ml) evaporated milk (not sweetened condensed milk)
- ¼ cup (60ml) milk (whole or 2%)
- 1 tsp vanilla extract

Instructions

1. Prepare the Pie Crust:

- In a medium bowl, whisk together the flour, granulated sugar, and salt.
- Cut in the cold butter using a pastry cutter or your fingers until the mixture resembles coarse crumbs with pea-sized pieces of butter.
- In a small bowl, whisk the egg yolk and add it to the flour mixture. Mix until combined.
- Gradually add ice water, one tablespoon at a time, until the dough just comes together.
- Form the dough into a disk, wrap in plastic wrap, and refrigerate for at least 30 minutes.

2. Preheat the Oven:

- Preheat your oven to 375°F (190°C).

3. Prepare the Sweet Potatoes:

- Peel and chop the sweet potatoes, then boil them in a pot of water until tender (about 15-20 minutes). Drain and mash until smooth. Alternatively, you can roast the sweet potatoes for more flavor: roast at 400°F (200°C) for 45-60 minutes until tender, then peel and mash.

4. Prepare the Filling:

- In a large bowl, combine the mashed sweet potatoes, granulated sugar, brown sugar, cinnamon, nutmeg, ginger, and salt. Mix well.
- Beat in the eggs, one at a time, until fully incorporated.
- Gradually add the evaporated milk, milk, and vanilla extract, mixing until smooth and well combined.

5. Roll Out the Dough:

- On a lightly floured surface, roll out the dough to about ⅛ inch (3 mm) thickness.
- Carefully transfer the dough to a 9-inch (23 cm) pie dish, gently pressing it into the edges. Trim any excess dough and crimp the edges if desired.
- Refrigerate the pie crust while preparing the filling.

6. Assemble the Pie:

- Pour the sweet potato filling into the prepared pie crust.

7. Bake the Pie:

- Bake in the preheated oven for 50-60 minutes, or until the filling is set and a knife inserted into the center comes out clean. The pie should be slightly puffed and firm to the touch.
- If the crust begins to brown too quickly, cover the edges with aluminum foil to prevent burning.

8. Cool and Serve:

- Allow the pie to cool completely on a wire rack before serving. The filling will firm up as it cools.
- Serve at room temperature or chilled. It's delicious on its own or with a dollop of whipped cream or a scoop of vanilla ice cream.

9. Store:

- Store the pie in an airtight container in the refrigerator for up to 5 days. It can also be frozen for up to 2 months. Thaw in the refrigerator before serving.

Sweet potato pie is a comforting and flavorful dessert that's perfect for holidays, special occasions, or just a cozy treat. Enjoy!

Maple Pecan Pie

Ingredients

For the Pie Crust:

- 1 ¼ cups (160g) all-purpose flour
- ¼ cup (50g) granulated sugar
- ¼ tsp salt
- ½ cup (115g) unsalted butter, cold and cut into small pieces
- 1 large egg yolk
- 2-4 tbsp ice water

For the Filling:

- 1 cup (240ml) pure maple syrup
- ½ cup (100g) granulated sugar
- ¼ cup (50g) packed light brown sugar
- ¼ cup (60g) unsalted butter, melted
- 3 large eggs
- 1 tsp vanilla extract
- 1 cup (120g) pecan halves
- ¼ tsp salt

Instructions

1. Prepare the Pie Crust:

- In a medium bowl, whisk together the flour, granulated sugar, and salt.
- Cut in the cold butter using a pastry cutter or your fingers until the mixture resembles coarse crumbs with pea-sized pieces of butter.
- In a small bowl, whisk the egg yolk and add it to the flour mixture. Mix until combined.
- Gradually add ice water, one tablespoon at a time, until the dough just comes together.
- Form the dough into a disk, wrap in plastic wrap, and refrigerate for at least 30 minutes.

2. Preheat the Oven:

- Preheat your oven to 350°F (175°C).

3. Roll Out the Dough:

- On a lightly floured surface, roll out the dough to about ⅛ inch (3 mm) thickness.
- Carefully transfer the dough to a 9-inch (23 cm) pie dish, gently pressing it into the edges. Trim any excess dough and crimp the edges if desired.
- Refrigerate the pie crust while preparing the filling.

4. Prepare the Filling:

- In a large bowl, whisk together the maple syrup, granulated sugar, brown sugar, melted butter, and salt until smooth.
- Beat in the eggs, one at a time, until fully incorporated.
- Stir in the vanilla extract.

5. Assemble the Pie:

- Arrange the pecan halves evenly over the bottom of the chilled pie crust.
- Pour the maple filling over the pecans, making sure they are evenly distributed.

6. Bake the Pie:

- Bake in the preheated oven for 50-60 minutes, or until the filling is set and a knife inserted into the center comes out clean. The pie should be slightly puffed and firm to the touch.
- If the crust begins to brown too quickly, cover the edges with aluminum foil to prevent burning.

7. Cool and Serve:

- Allow the pie to cool completely on a wire rack before serving. The filling will firm up as it cools.
- Serve at room temperature or slightly warmed. It's delicious on its own or with a dollop of whipped cream or a scoop of vanilla ice cream.

8. Store:

- Store the pie in an airtight container in the refrigerator for up to 5 days. It can also be frozen for up to 2 months. Thaw in the refrigerator before serving.

This maple pecan pie offers a rich and distinctive flavor with the warm notes of maple syrup and crunchy pecans. It's a perfect dessert for special occasions, holidays, or any time you want to enjoy a comforting, sweet treat. Enjoy!

Chocolate Gingerbread Cupcakes

Ingredients

For the Cupcakes:

- 1 ½ cups (190g) all-purpose flour
- ¾ cup (65g) unsweetened cocoa powder
- 1 tsp baking powder
- 1 tsp baking soda
- ½ tsp salt
- 1 tsp ground ginger
- 1 tsp ground cinnamon
- ¼ tsp ground cloves
- ¼ tsp ground nutmeg
- ¾ cup (150g) granulated sugar
- ½ cup (100g) packed brown sugar
- ½ cup (115g) unsalted butter, softened
- 2 large eggs
- ½ cup (120ml) buttermilk
- ½ cup (120ml) molasses
- 1 tsp vanilla extract

For the Gingerbread Cream Cheese Frosting:

- 8 oz (225g) cream cheese, softened
- ½ cup (115g) unsalted butter, softened
- 4 cups (480g) powdered sugar
- 1 tsp ground ginger
- 1 tsp ground cinnamon
- ¼ tsp ground cloves
- ¼ tsp ground nutmeg
- 1-2 tbsp milk or heavy cream (for desired consistency)
- Optional: Crystallized ginger pieces for garnish

Instructions

1. Preheat the Oven:

- Preheat your oven to 350°F (175°C). Line a 12-cup muffin tin with paper liners.

2. Mix Dry Ingredients:

- In a medium bowl, whisk together the flour, cocoa powder, baking powder, baking soda, salt, ginger, cinnamon, cloves, and nutmeg.

3. Cream Butter and Sugars:

- In a large bowl, cream together the softened butter, granulated sugar, and brown sugar until light and fluffy.

4. Add Eggs and Wet Ingredients:

- Beat in the eggs, one at a time, until fully incorporated.
- Add the molasses and vanilla extract, mixing until combined.

5. Combine Dry and Wet Ingredients:

- Gradually add the dry ingredients to the wet ingredients, alternating with the buttermilk. Begin and end with the dry ingredients, mixing until just combined. Avoid overmixing.

6. Fill Cupcake Liners:

- Divide the batter evenly among the 12 cupcake liners, filling each about ⅔ full.

7. Bake:

- Bake in the preheated oven for 18-22 minutes, or until a toothpick inserted into the center comes out clean.
- Allow the cupcakes to cool in the tin for 5 minutes, then transfer them to a wire rack to cool completely before frosting.

8. Prepare the Frosting:

- In a large bowl, beat the softened cream cheese and butter together until creamy.
- Gradually add the powdered sugar, one cup at a time, beating well after each addition.
- Add the ground ginger, cinnamon, cloves, and nutmeg. Beat until smooth and well combined.
- Adjust the consistency with milk or heavy cream as needed.

9. Frost the Cupcakes:

- Once the cupcakes are completely cooled, frost them with the gingerbread cream cheese frosting using a piping bag or a spatula.
- Garnish with pieces of crystallized ginger if desired.

10. Store:

- Store the frosted cupcakes in an airtight container in the refrigerator for up to 3 days. Allow them to come to room temperature before serving for the best flavor.

These chocolate gingerbread cupcakes are a wonderful blend of rich chocolate and warm spices, perfect for holiday gatherings or as a special treat any time of year. Enjoy!

Coconut Macaroons

Ingredients

- 2 ½ cups (200g) sweetened shredded coconut
- 1 cup (240ml) sweetened condensed milk
- 1 tsp vanilla extract
- ¼ tsp almond extract (optional, for added flavor)
- A pinch of salt
- 2 large egg whites
- ¼ tsp cream of tartar
- ¼ cup (50g) granulated sugar (for beating with egg whites)

For Drizzling (optional):

- 4 oz (115g) semisweet or bittersweet chocolate, chopped

Instructions

1. Preheat the Oven:

- Preheat your oven to 325°F (160°C). Line a baking sheet with parchment paper or a silicone baking mat.

2. Prepare the Coconut Mixture:

- In a large bowl, combine the shredded coconut, sweetened condensed milk, vanilla extract, almond extract (if using), and a pinch of salt. Mix until well combined.

3. Whip the Egg Whites:

- In a clean, dry mixing bowl, beat the egg whites with an electric mixer on medium speed until they start to froth.
- Add the cream of tartar and continue beating until soft peaks form.
- Gradually add the granulated sugar while beating, until the egg whites form stiff, glossy peaks.

4. Fold in the Egg Whites:

- Gently fold the whipped egg whites into the coconut mixture in three additions. Be careful not to deflate the egg whites too much; fold just until the mixture is combined and no streaks remain.

5. Scoop the Macaroons:

- Using a cookie scoop or a tablespoon, drop rounded mounds of the coconut mixture onto the prepared baking sheet. Space them about 1 inch (2.5 cm) apart. You can shape them into small pyramids or leave them as mounds.

6. Bake:

- Bake in the preheated oven for 15-20 minutes, or until the macaroons are golden brown around the edges and on top.
- Remove from the oven and let them cool on the baking sheet for about 5 minutes before transferring to a wire rack to cool completely.

7. Optional Chocolate Drizzle:

- If desired, melt the chopped chocolate in a microwave-safe bowl or over a double boiler until smooth.
- Drizzle the melted chocolate over the cooled macaroons using a fork or spoon. Allow the chocolate to set before serving.

8. Store:

- Store the macaroons in an airtight container at room temperature for up to 1 week. They can also be frozen for up to 3 months. Thaw at room temperature before serving.

Coconut macaroons are perfect for any occasion, from casual snacks to festive treats. Their simple, sweet flavor and chewy texture make them a favorite for coconut lovers. Enjoy!

Eggnog Pound Cake

Ingredients

For the Cake:

- 2 ½ cups (320g) all-purpose flour
- 1 ½ tsp baking powder
- ¼ tsp salt
- 1 cup (230g) unsalted butter, softened
- 1 ½ cups (300g) granulated sugar
- 4 large eggs
- 1 cup (240ml) eggnog
- 2 tbsp (30ml) rum or bourbon (optional, for added flavor)
- 1 tsp vanilla extract
- 1 tsp ground nutmeg
- ¼ tsp ground cinnamon

For the Glaze (optional):

- 1 cup (120g) powdered sugar
- 2-3 tbsp milk or eggnog
- ¼ tsp ground nutmeg
- Optional: 1 tbsp (15ml) rum or bourbon

Instructions

1. Preheat the Oven:

- Preheat your oven to 325°F (163°C). Grease and flour a 10-cup bundt pan or a 9x5-inch (23x13 cm) loaf pan.

2. Mix Dry Ingredients:

- In a medium bowl, whisk together the flour, baking powder, salt, ground nutmeg, and ground cinnamon.

3. Cream Butter and Sugar:

- In a large bowl, beat the softened butter and granulated sugar together until light and fluffy.

4. Add Eggs and Flavors:

- Beat in the eggs, one at a time, until fully incorporated.
- Mix in the vanilla extract and, if using, the rum or bourbon.

5. Combine Wet and Dry Ingredients:

- Gradually add the dry ingredients to the butter mixture, alternating with the eggnog. Begin and end with the dry ingredients, mixing until just combined. Do not overmix.

6. Pour Batter into Pan:

- Pour the batter into the prepared bundt pan or loaf pan, smoothing the top with a spatula.

7. Bake the Cake:

- Bake in the preheated oven for 60-75 minutes, or until a toothpick inserted into the center comes out clean and the cake is golden brown.
- If baking in a loaf pan, the baking time may be closer to 60 minutes; check for doneness early.

8. Cool the Cake:

- Allow the cake to cool in the pan for 15 minutes before transferring to a wire rack to cool completely.

9. Prepare the Glaze (if using):

- In a small bowl, whisk together the powdered sugar, milk or eggnog, ground nutmeg, and optional rum or bourbon until smooth and well combined.
- Drizzle the glaze over the cooled cake.

10. Serve and Store:

- Serve the cake at room temperature. It can be stored in an airtight container at room temperature for up to 5 days, or in the refrigerator for up to 1 week. The cake can also be frozen for up to 3 months; thaw at room temperature before serving.

This eggnog pound cake is a wonderful way to enjoy the flavors of the season in a rich, moist cake. It pairs beautifully with a cup of coffee or tea and is sure to be a hit at holiday gatherings. Enjoy!

Toffee Crunch Bars

Ingredients

For the Crust:

- 1 ½ cups (190g) all-purpose flour
- ½ cup (100g) granulated sugar
- ½ cup (115g) unsalted butter, cold and cut into small pieces
- ¼ tsp salt

For the Toffee Layer:

- 1 cup (200g) packed brown sugar
- ½ cup (115g) unsalted butter
- 2 tbsp light corn syrup
- ¼ tsp salt

For the Topping:

- 1 cup (170g) semisweet or milk chocolate chips
- ½ cup (50g) chopped nuts (such as pecans, walnuts, or almonds)
- ½ cup (50g) toffee bits (optional, for extra crunch)

Instructions

1. Preheat the Oven:

- Preheat your oven to 350°F (175°C). Grease an 8x8-inch (20x20 cm) baking pan or line it with parchment paper.

2. Prepare the Crust:

- In a medium bowl, combine the flour, granulated sugar, and salt.
- Cut in the cold butter using a pastry cutter or your fingers until the mixture resembles coarse crumbs.
- Press the mixture evenly into the bottom of the prepared baking pan to form the crust.

3. Bake the Crust:

- Bake in the preheated oven for 15 minutes, or until lightly golden.

4. Prepare the Toffee Layer:

- While the crust is baking, in a medium saucepan over medium heat, combine the brown sugar, butter, corn syrup, and salt.

- Stir constantly until the mixture comes to a boil, then continue to cook for 3-4 minutes, stirring frequently, until it thickens slightly.
- Remove from heat.

5. Assemble the Bars:

- Pour the toffee mixture evenly over the baked crust, spreading it to cover the surface.

6. Bake Again:

- Return the pan to the oven and bake for an additional 10 minutes, or until the toffee layer is bubbly and golden.

7. Add the Topping:

- Remove from the oven and immediately sprinkle the chocolate chips evenly over the hot toffee layer.
- Allow the chocolate chips to soften for a few minutes, then spread the melted chocolate evenly over the top with a spatula.
- Sprinkle the chopped nuts and toffee bits (if using) over the melted chocolate, pressing them lightly into the chocolate.

8. Cool and Cut:

- Allow the bars to cool completely in the pan on a wire rack. The chocolate will need to set, which may take 1-2 hours at room temperature, or you can speed up the process by refrigerating them.
- Once cooled and set, lift the bars out of the pan using the parchment paper (if used) and cut into squares or bars.

9. Store:

- Store the toffee crunch bars in an airtight container at room temperature for up to 1 week. They can also be refrigerated for longer shelf life or frozen for up to 2 months.

These toffee crunch bars are a wonderful mix of textures and flavors, with a buttery crust, sweet toffee, and rich chocolate. They're sure to be a hit wherever you serve them! Enjoy!

Spiced Nuts

Ingredients

- 2 cups (250g) mixed nuts (such as almonds, cashews, pecans, walnuts, or hazelnuts)
- 2 tbsp olive oil or melted butter
- 1 tbsp maple syrup or honey
- 1 tsp smoked paprika
- 1 tsp ground cumin
- 1 tsp ground coriander
- ½ tsp ground cinnamon
- ½ tsp ground turmeric (optional, for color and flavor)
- ¼ tsp cayenne pepper (adjust to taste for heat)
- 1 tsp kosher salt
- ½ tsp ground black pepper
- 2 tbsp fresh rosemary or thyme, finely chopped (optional, for a herby flavor)

Instructions

1. Preheat the Oven:

- Preheat your oven to 350°F (175°C). Line a baking sheet with parchment paper or a silicone baking mat.

2. Prepare the Nuts:

- In a large bowl, combine the mixed nuts with olive oil or melted butter and maple syrup or honey. Toss to coat the nuts evenly.

3. Mix the Spices:

- In a small bowl, mix together the smoked paprika, ground cumin, ground coriander, ground cinnamon, ground turmeric (if using), cayenne pepper, kosher salt, and black pepper.

4. Season the Nuts:

- Sprinkle the spice mixture over the coated nuts and toss well to ensure an even coating. If using fresh rosemary or thyme, stir it in at this point.

5. Roast the Nuts:

- Spread the seasoned nuts in a single layer on the prepared baking sheet.
- Roast in the preheated oven for 12-15 minutes, stirring halfway through, until the nuts are golden brown and fragrant. Watch carefully to avoid burning.

6. Cool and Store:

- Remove the nuts from the oven and let them cool completely on the baking sheet. They will become crisp as they cool.
- Store the spiced nuts in an airtight container at room temperature for up to 2 weeks. For longer storage, keep them in the refrigerator for up to a month or freeze for up to 3 months.

7. Variations:

- Feel free to customize the spice blend to suit your tastes. You can add a pinch of chili powder for extra heat, a bit of brown sugar for sweetness, or other herbs and spices like garlic powder or onion powder for additional flavor profiles.

These spiced nuts are crunchy, savory, and slightly sweet, making them an addictive snack that's perfect for any occasion. Enjoy!

Holiday Thumbprint Cookies

Ingredients

For the Cookies:

- 1 cup (230g) unsalted butter, softened
- ½ cup (100g) granulated sugar
- ¼ cup (50g) packed brown sugar
- 1 large egg yolk
- 2 tsp vanilla extract
- 2 cups (240g) all-purpose flour
- ¼ tsp salt
- ½ tsp baking powder

For the Filling:

- ½ cup (160g) fruit preserves or jam (such as raspberry, apricot, or strawberry)
- Optional: a few drops of lemon juice (to thin out the jam if needed)

For Rolling (optional):

- ¼ cup (50g) granulated sugar
- ¼ cup (25g) finely chopped nuts (such as walnuts, pecans, or almonds)

Instructions

1. Preheat the Oven:

- Preheat your oven to 350°F (175°C). Line two baking sheets with parchment paper or silicone baking mats.

2. Prepare the Dough:

- In a large bowl, cream together the softened butter, granulated sugar, and brown sugar until light and fluffy.
- Beat in the egg yolk and vanilla extract until well combined.
- In a separate bowl, whisk together the flour, salt, and baking powder.
- Gradually add the dry ingredients to the butter mixture, mixing until just combined.

3. Shape the Cookies:

- Roll the dough into 1-inch (2.5 cm) balls and place them about 2 inches (5 cm) apart on the prepared baking sheets.
- Using your thumb or the back of a small spoon, make an indentation in the center of each dough ball. Be careful not to press too hard; you want a deep enough well to hold the filling, but not so deep that the cookie spreads too thin.

4. Add the Filling:

- Spoon a small amount of fruit preserves or jam into each indentation. If the jam is too thick, you can thin it out with a few drops of lemon juice.

5. Optional Rolling:

- If desired, roll the edges of the cookies in granulated sugar and finely chopped nuts before baking. This adds a nice crunch and extra flavor to the cookies.

6. Bake:

- Bake in the preheated oven for 12-15 minutes, or until the edges of the cookies are lightly golden.
- Allow the cookies to cool on the baking sheets for about 5 minutes before transferring them to a wire rack to cool completely.

7. Store:

- Store the thumbprint cookies in an airtight container at room temperature for up to 1 week. They can also be frozen for up to 3 months; thaw at room temperature before serving.

8. Variations:

- You can use different flavors of jam or preserves to suit your taste. Consider adding a bit of lemon zest to the cookie dough for a fresh citrus twist or sprinkling a little powdered sugar on top of the cooled cookies for an extra festive touch.

Holiday thumbprint cookies are not only delicious but also visually appealing, making them a great addition to any holiday cookie platter. Enjoy baking and sharing these festive treats!

Dark Chocolate Cranberry Tart

Ingredients

For the Tart Crust:

- 1 ¼ cups (160g) all-purpose flour
- ¼ cup (50g) granulated sugar
- ¼ tsp salt
- ½ cup (115g) unsalted butter, cold and cut into small pieces
- 1 large egg yolk
- 1-2 tbsp ice water (as needed)

For the Chocolate Filling:

- 1 cup (240ml) heavy cream
- 8 oz (225g) dark chocolate, chopped (70% cocoa recommended)
- 2 tbsp unsalted butter
- 1 tsp vanilla extract

For the Cranberry Topping:

- 1 cup (120g) fresh cranberries
- ½ cup (100g) granulated sugar
- ¼ cup (60ml) water
- 1 tsp orange zest (optional)
- 1 tbsp fresh lemon juice

For Garnish (optional):

- Fresh mint leaves
- Shaved chocolate or cocoa powder

Instructions

1. Prepare the Tart Crust:

- In a medium bowl, whisk together the flour, granulated sugar, and salt.
- Cut in the cold butter using a pastry cutter or your fingers until the mixture resembles coarse crumbs.
- In a small bowl, whisk the egg yolk and add it to the flour mixture. Mix until combined.
- Gradually add ice water, one tablespoon at a time, until the dough just comes together. Form the dough into a disk, wrap in plastic wrap, and refrigerate for at least 30 minutes.

2. Preheat the Oven:

- Preheat your oven to 350°F (175°C).

3. Roll Out and Bake the Crust:

- On a lightly floured surface, roll out the dough to fit a 9-inch (23 cm) tart pan with a removable bottom. Press the dough into the tart pan, trimming any excess.
- Line the crust with parchment paper and fill with pie weights or dried beans.
- Bake in the preheated oven for 15 minutes. Remove the parchment paper and weights, and bake for an additional 5 minutes, or until the crust is lightly golden. Allow to cool completely.

4. Prepare the Chocolate Filling:

- In a medium saucepan, heat the heavy cream over medium heat until it just begins to simmer.
- Remove from heat and add the chopped dark chocolate. Let it sit for 2-3 minutes to melt.
- Stir until the chocolate is completely melted and smooth. Add the unsalted butter and vanilla extract, stirring until the butter is melted and fully incorporated.
- Pour the chocolate filling into the cooled tart crust, smoothing the top with a spatula. Refrigerate until the filling is set, about 1-2 hours.

5. Prepare the Cranberry Topping:

- In a medium saucepan, combine the fresh cranberries, granulated sugar, water, and orange zest (if using). Bring to a boil, then reduce the heat and simmer for 10 minutes, or until the cranberries burst and the mixture thickens.
- Stir in the lemon juice and remove from heat. Let the cranberry topping cool to room temperature.

6. Assemble the Tart:

- Once the chocolate filling is set, spread the cranberry topping evenly over the chocolate layer.

7. Garnish and Serve:

- Garnish with fresh mint leaves and shaved chocolate or a dusting of cocoa powder if desired.
- Serve chilled or at room temperature.

8. Store:

- Store any leftover tart in the refrigerator for up to 3 days. The tart can also be frozen for up to 1 month; thaw in the refrigerator before serving.

This Dark Chocolate Cranberry Tart combines the richness of dark chocolate with the vibrant tartness of cranberries, making for a stunning and delectable dessert. Enjoy!

Cinnamon Roll Casserole

Ingredients

For the Casserole:

- 2 cans (16 oz each) refrigerated cinnamon rolls with icing (8 rolls per can)
- 4 large eggs
- 1 cup (240ml) whole milk
- ½ cup (120ml) heavy cream
- 1 tsp vanilla extract
- 1 tsp ground cinnamon
- ¼ tsp ground nutmeg
- ¼ cup (50g) granulated sugar (optional, for extra sweetness)
- ½ cup (75g) chopped pecans or walnuts (optional)

For the Glaze:

- 1 cup (120g) powdered sugar
- 2 tbsp milk or heavy cream
- ½ tsp vanilla extract

Instructions

1. Preheat the Oven:

- Preheat your oven to 350°F (175°C). Grease a 9x13-inch (23x33 cm) baking dish or spray it with non-stick cooking spray.

2. Prepare the Cinnamon Rolls:

- Open the cans of refrigerated cinnamon rolls. Set aside the icing that comes with the rolls.
- Cut each cinnamon roll into quarters and place them in the prepared baking dish. If using nuts, sprinkle them over the cinnamon rolls.

3. Make the Egg Mixture:

- In a large bowl, whisk together the eggs, milk, heavy cream, vanilla extract, ground cinnamon, nutmeg, and granulated sugar (if using).

4. Assemble the Casserole:

- Pour the egg mixture evenly over the cinnamon rolls in the baking dish, making sure to cover all the pieces.

5. Bake:

- Bake in the preheated oven for 30-35 minutes, or until the casserole is set in the center and the top is golden brown.

6. Prepare the Glaze:

- While the casserole is baking, make the glaze by whisking together the powdered sugar, milk or heavy cream, and vanilla extract in a small bowl until smooth.

7. Glaze the Casserole:

- Once the casserole is baked, remove it from the oven and let it cool for a few minutes.
- Drizzle the prepared glaze evenly over the warm casserole.

8. Serve:

- Cut the casserole into squares and serve warm.

9. Store:

- Store any leftovers in an airtight container in the refrigerator for up to 3 days. Reheat individual portions in the microwave or oven before serving.

This cinnamon roll casserole is perfect for a cozy breakfast or brunch, and it's a great way to enjoy the flavors of cinnamon rolls with minimal effort. Enjoy!

Peppermint Mocha Brownies

Ingredients

For the Brownies:

- ½ cup (115g) unsalted butter
- 1 cup (200g) granulated sugar
- 2 large eggs
- 1 tsp vanilla extract
- ⅓ cup (40g) unsweetened cocoa powder
- ½ cup (60g) all-purpose flour
- ¼ tsp salt
- ¼ tsp baking powder
- 1 cup (170g) semisweet chocolate chips
- 1 tbsp instant coffee granules (or espresso powder)
- ¼ cup (60ml) boiling water

For the Peppermint Swirl:

- ½ cup (120ml) heavy cream
- 1 cup (170g) semisweet chocolate chips
- ½ tsp peppermint extract
- Crushed candy canes or peppermint candies for garnish

Instructions

1. Preheat the Oven:

- Preheat your oven to 350°F (175°C). Grease and flour an 8x8-inch (20x20 cm) baking pan or line it with parchment paper.

2. Prepare the Brownie Batter:

- In a medium saucepan over low heat, melt the butter. Remove from heat and stir in the granulated sugar, eggs, and vanilla extract.
- Beat in the cocoa powder until smooth.
- Stir in the flour, salt, and baking powder until just combined.
- In a small bowl, dissolve the instant coffee granules in the boiling water. Stir the coffee mixture into the brownie batter.
- Fold in the semisweet chocolate chips.

3. Bake the Brownies:

- Pour the brownie batter into the prepared baking pan and spread it evenly.

- Bake in the preheated oven for 25-30 minutes, or until a toothpick inserted into the center comes out with a few moist crumbs. The brownies should be set but still fudgy.

4. Prepare the Peppermint Swirl:

- While the brownies are baking, make the peppermint swirl. In a small saucepan, heat the heavy cream over medium heat until it just begins to simmer.
- Remove from heat and add the chocolate chips. Let sit for 2-3 minutes, then stir until smooth and shiny.
- Stir in the peppermint extract.

5. Swirl the Peppermint Ganache:

- As soon as the brownies come out of the oven, pour the peppermint ganache over the warm brownies. Use a knife or skewer to swirl the ganache into the brownie batter for a marbled effect.

6. Garnish and Cool:

- Sprinkle crushed candy canes or peppermint candies over the top while the ganache is still soft.
- Allow the brownies to cool completely in the pan on a wire rack before cutting into squares.

7. Store:

- Store the brownies in an airtight container at room temperature for up to 1 week. They can also be frozen for up to 3 months; thaw at room temperature before serving.

These peppermint mocha brownies are rich, chocolatey, and have a delightful peppermint twist, making them an irresistible treat for any occasion! Enjoy!

Fig and Walnut Cookies

Ingredients

For the Dough:

- 1 cup (230g) unsalted butter, softened
- 1 cup (200g) granulated sugar
- 1 large egg
- 1 tsp vanilla extract
- 2 ¼ cups (280g) all-purpose flour
- ½ tsp baking soda
- ½ tsp baking powder
- ¼ tsp salt

For the Filling:

- 1 cup (150g) dried figs, chopped
- ½ cup (60g) chopped walnuts
- ¼ cup (60ml) orange juice (or water)
- 2 tbsp granulated sugar
- ½ tsp ground cinnamon
- ¼ tsp ground cloves

Instructions

1. Prepare the Filling:

- In a small saucepan, combine the chopped figs, chopped walnuts, orange juice, granulated sugar, ground cinnamon, and ground cloves.
- Cook over medium heat, stirring frequently, until the mixture thickens and the figs become soft, about 5-7 minutes.
- Remove from heat and let it cool completely. The filling will continue to thicken as it cools.

2. Prepare the Dough:

- In a large bowl, cream together the softened butter and granulated sugar until light and fluffy.
- Beat in the egg and vanilla extract until well combined.
- In a separate bowl, whisk together the flour, baking soda, baking powder, and salt.
- Gradually add the dry ingredients to the butter mixture, mixing until just combined.

3. Assemble the Cookies:

- Preheat your oven to 350°F (175°C). Line a baking sheet with parchment paper.

- Scoop about 1 tablespoon of dough and flatten it slightly in your hand. Place a small spoonful of the fig filling in the center.
- Fold the edges of the dough around the filling, pinching the dough to seal it completely. Roll the filled dough into a ball and place it on the prepared baking sheet.
- Flatten each cookie slightly with your hand or the bottom of a glass.

4. Bake:

- Bake in the preheated oven for 12-15 minutes, or until the edges are lightly golden.
- Allow the cookies to cool on the baking sheet for a few minutes before transferring them to a wire rack to cool completely.

5. Store:

- Store the cookies in an airtight container at room temperature for up to 1 week. They can also be frozen for up to 3 months; thaw at room temperature before serving.

6. Optional Glaze:

- For a finishing touch, you can drizzle the cooled cookies with a simple glaze made from powdered sugar and a little milk, or sprinkle them with a bit of powdered sugar.

These fig and walnut cookies are a wonderful combination of sweet and nutty flavors, with a satisfying chewy texture. They're sure to be a hit with anyone who tries them! Enjoy!

Classic Fruit and Nut Cake

Ingredients

For the Cake:

- 1 cup (230g) unsalted butter, softened
- 1 cup (200g) granulated sugar
- 4 large eggs
- 1 cup (240ml) orange juice
- 2 tsp vanilla extract
- 2 ½ cups (300g) all-purpose flour
- 1 tsp baking powder
- 1 tsp baking soda
- ½ tsp salt
- 1 tsp ground cinnamon
- ½ tsp ground nutmeg
- ¼ tsp ground cloves

For the Fruit and Nut Mix:

- 1 cup (150g) chopped dried apricots
- 1 cup (150g) chopped dried figs
- 1 cup (150g) chopped dried dates
- 1 cup (150g) raisins or currants
- 1 cup (120g) chopped walnuts
- 1 cup (120g) chopped pecans
- ½ cup (75g) chopped almonds
- 1 cup (150g) candied cherries (optional)
- ½ cup (75g) chopped crystallized ginger (optional)
- 1 cup (240ml) dark rum or orange juice (for soaking the fruit, optional)

For the Glaze (optional):

- ½ cup (120ml) apricot preserves or jam
- 1 tbsp water

Instructions

1. Prepare the Fruit and Nut Mix:

- If using, soak the dried fruit in dark rum or orange juice for at least 2 hours or overnight to plump them up. Drain well and pat dry with paper towels.
- In a large bowl, combine the soaked dried fruit with the chopped nuts, candied cherries, and crystallized ginger. Toss to mix evenly.

2. Preheat the Oven:

- Preheat your oven to 325°F (165°C). Grease and flour a 9x13-inch (23x33 cm) baking pan, or line it with parchment paper. For a more traditional look, you can use two 8-inch (20 cm) round pans.

3. Prepare the Cake Batter:

- In a large bowl, cream together the softened butter and granulated sugar until light and fluffy.
- Beat in the eggs, one at a time, until well incorporated.
- Mix in the orange juice and vanilla extract.
- In another bowl, whisk together the flour, baking powder, baking soda, salt, ground cinnamon, nutmeg, and cloves.
- Gradually add the dry ingredients to the wet ingredients, mixing until just combined.

4. Fold in the Fruit and Nut Mix:

- Gently fold the fruit and nut mixture into the batter until evenly distributed.

5. Bake the Cake:

- Pour the batter into the prepared baking pan and spread it evenly.
- Bake in the preheated oven for 50-60 minutes, or until a toothpick inserted into the center comes out clean. If using round pans, check for doneness after 35-40 minutes.

6. Cool and Glaze (Optional):

- Allow the cake to cool in the pan for 10 minutes before transferring it to a wire rack to cool completely.
- If desired, heat the apricot preserves with water until melted and smooth. Brush the glaze over the cooled cake for a shiny finish.

7. Store:

- Store the fruit and nut cake in an airtight container at room temperature for up to 1 week. It also improves in flavor as it sits. For longer storage, wrap tightly and freeze for up to 3 months; thaw at room temperature before serving.

This classic fruit and nut cake is a festive, rich, and satisfying treat that's perfect for holiday celebrations or any special occasion. Enjoy!

Apple Streusel Bars

Ingredients

For the Crust:

- 1 cup (230g) unsalted butter, softened
- ½ cup (100g) granulated sugar
- ½ cup (100g) packed brown sugar
- 2 large eggs
- 1 tsp vanilla extract
- 2 ¼ cups (280g) all-purpose flour
- 1 tsp baking powder
- ¼ tsp salt

For the Apple Filling:

- 4 cups (about 4 medium) peeled and thinly sliced apples (such as Granny Smith or Honeycrisp)
- ⅓ cup (65g) granulated sugar
- 1 tbsp lemon juice
- 1 tsp ground cinnamon
- ¼ tsp ground nutmeg
- 2 tbsp all-purpose flour

For the Streusel Topping:

- ½ cup (115g) unsalted butter, cold and cut into small pieces
- ½ cup (100g) granulated sugar
- ½ cup (100g) packed brown sugar
- 1 cup (120g) all-purpose flour
- ½ cup (50g) old-fashioned rolled oats
- ½ tsp ground cinnamon

Instructions

1. Prepare the Crust:

- Preheat your oven to 350°F (175°C). Grease and flour a 9x13-inch (23x33 cm) baking dish or line it with parchment paper.

2. Mix the Crust Dough:

- In a large bowl, cream together the softened butter, granulated sugar, and brown sugar until light and fluffy.
- Beat in the eggs one at a time, then add the vanilla extract and mix well.

- In another bowl, whisk together the flour, baking powder, and salt.
- Gradually add the dry ingredients to the wet ingredients, mixing until just combined.

3. Bake the Crust:

- Press about 2/3 of the dough into the bottom of the prepared baking dish to form an even layer.
- Bake in the preheated oven for 10-12 minutes, or until lightly golden. Remove from the oven and set aside.

4. Prepare the Apple Filling:

- While the crust is baking, toss the sliced apples with granulated sugar, lemon juice, ground cinnamon, ground nutmeg, and flour in a large bowl until well coated.

5. Prepare the Streusel Topping:

- In a medium bowl, combine the cold butter, granulated sugar, brown sugar, flour, rolled oats, and ground cinnamon.
- Use a pastry cutter or your fingers to work the butter into the dry ingredients until the mixture resembles coarse crumbs.

6. Assemble the Bars:

- Spread the apple filling evenly over the pre-baked crust.
- Sprinkle the streusel topping evenly over the apple filling.

7. Bake the Bars:

- Return the pan to the oven and bake for 35-45 minutes, or until the topping is golden brown and the apple filling is bubbling.

8. Cool and Serve:

- Allow the bars to cool completely in the pan on a wire rack before cutting into squares.
- Serve at room temperature or slightly warmed, with a scoop of vanilla ice cream or a dollop of whipped cream if desired.

9. Store:

- Store any leftover bars in an airtight container at room temperature for up to 4 days. They can also be refrigerated for up to a week or frozen for up to 3 months; thaw before serving.

These apple streusel bars are a delightful combination of textures and flavors, making them a perfect treat for any occasion. Enjoy!

Chocolate Mint Pie

Ingredients

For the Crust:

- 1 ½ cups (150g) chocolate cookie crumbs (such as Oreo or other chocolate sandwich cookies)
- ¼ cup (50g) granulated sugar
- 6 tbsp (85g) unsalted butter, melted

For the Chocolate Mint Filling:

- 1 cup (240ml) heavy cream
- 8 oz (225g) semisweet chocolate, chopped
- ½ cup (120ml) peppermint or mint-flavored creamer (or milk, if you prefer)
- 2 large eggs
- ¼ cup (50g) granulated sugar
- 1 tsp peppermint extract

For the Whipped Cream Topping:

- 1 cup (240ml) heavy cream
- 2 tbsp powdered sugar
- ½ tsp vanilla extract

For Garnish (optional):

- Crushed chocolate cookies or mint chocolate chips
- Fresh mint leaves

Instructions

1. Prepare the Crust:

- Preheat your oven to 350°F (175°C).
- In a medium bowl, combine the chocolate cookie crumbs and granulated sugar.
- Pour in the melted butter and mix until the crumbs are evenly coated.
- Press the mixture firmly into the bottom and up the sides of a 9-inch (23 cm) pie pan to form an even crust.
- Bake in the preheated oven for 10 minutes. Remove from the oven and let it cool completely.

2. Prepare the Chocolate Mint Filling:

- In a medium saucepan, heat the heavy cream over medium heat until it just begins to simmer. Remove from heat.

- Add the chopped semisweet chocolate to the hot cream and let it sit for 2-3 minutes to melt. Stir until smooth.
- Stir in the peppermint or mint-flavored creamer (or milk) until well combined.
- In a separate bowl, whisk together the eggs and granulated sugar until light and frothy.
- Gradually add the chocolate mixture to the egg mixture, whisking constantly to combine.
- Stir in the peppermint extract.

3. Fill the Pie Crust:

- Pour the chocolate mint filling into the cooled pie crust, spreading it evenly.
- Bake in the preheated oven for 20-25 minutes, or until the filling is set around the edges but still slightly jiggly in the center.
- Allow the pie to cool to room temperature, then refrigerate for at least 4 hours or until completely chilled and set.

4. Prepare the Whipped Cream Topping:

- In a medium bowl, beat the heavy cream, powdered sugar, and vanilla extract with an electric mixer until soft peaks form.
- Spread or pipe the whipped cream over the chilled pie.

5. Garnish and Serve:

- Garnish with crushed chocolate cookies, mint chocolate chips, or fresh mint leaves if desired.
- Slice and serve chilled.

6. Store:

- Store any leftover pie in the refrigerator for up to 5 days. The pie can also be frozen for up to 3 months; thaw in the refrigerator before serving.

This chocolate mint pie is a rich, creamy, and refreshing dessert that combines the best of both chocolate and mint flavors. Enjoy!

Raspberry Almond Bars

Ingredients

For the Crust and Crumb Topping:

- 1 ½ cups (190g) all-purpose flour
- ½ cup (100g) granulated sugar
- ½ tsp baking powder
- ¼ tsp salt
- ½ cup (115g) unsalted butter, cold and cut into small pieces
- ½ cup (60g) sliced almonds

For the Raspberry Filling:

- 2 cups (240g) fresh or frozen raspberries
- ½ cup (100g) granulated sugar
- 1 tbsp cornstarch
- 1 tbsp lemon juice
- ¼ tsp vanilla extract

For Garnish (optional):

- Powdered sugar for dusting
- Extra sliced almonds for topping

Instructions

1. Prepare the Raspberry Filling:

- In a medium saucepan, combine the raspberries, granulated sugar, cornstarch, lemon juice, and vanilla extract.
- Cook over medium heat, stirring frequently, until the mixture starts to bubble and thicken, about 5-7 minutes.
- Remove from heat and let it cool to room temperature. It will continue to thicken as it cools.

2. Prepare the Crust and Crumb Topping:

- Preheat your oven to 350°F (175°C). Grease and flour an 8x8-inch (20x20 cm) baking dish or line it with parchment paper.
- In a medium bowl, whisk together the flour, granulated sugar, baking powder, and salt.
- Cut in the cold butter using a pastry cutter or your fingers until the mixture resembles coarse crumbs.
- Stir in the sliced almonds.

- Reserve 1 cup of the crumb mixture for the topping. Press the remaining crumb mixture evenly into the bottom of the prepared baking dish to form the crust.

3. Assemble the Bars:

- Spread the raspberry filling evenly over the pre-baked crust.
- Sprinkle the reserved crumb mixture evenly over the raspberry filling.
- Optionally, sprinkle a few extra sliced almonds on top.

4. Bake:

- Bake in the preheated oven for 30-35 minutes, or until the top is golden brown and the filling is bubbling.

5. Cool and Serve:

- Allow the bars to cool completely in the pan on a wire rack before cutting into squares.
- Dust with powdered sugar if desired before serving.

6. Store:

- Store the raspberry almond bars in an airtight container at room temperature for up to 5 days. They can also be refrigerated for up to a week or frozen for up to 3 months; thaw before serving.

These raspberry almond bars are a delicious blend of sweet and tart, with a satisfying crunch from the almonds. Enjoy them as a delightful treat any time of year!

Poppy Seed Loaf

Ingredients

For the Loaf:

- 1 ¾ cups (220g) all-purpose flour
- 1 cup (200g) granulated sugar
- 1 tsp baking powder
- ¼ tsp salt
- ½ cup (115g) unsalted butter, softened
- 3 large eggs
- ½ cup (120ml) milk (whole or 2%)
- 1 tbsp poppy seeds
- 1 tsp vanilla extract
- 1 tsp lemon zest (optional, for added flavor)
- 2 tbsp lemon juice (optional, for added flavor)

For the Glaze (optional):

- 1 cup (120g) powdered sugar
- 2-3 tbsp lemon juice (or milk) to thin

Instructions

1. Preheat the Oven:

- Preheat your oven to 350°F (175°C). Grease and flour a 9x5-inch (23x13 cm) loaf pan, or line it with parchment paper.

2. Prepare the Batter:

- In a medium bowl, whisk together the flour, granulated sugar, baking powder, and salt.
- In a large bowl, cream together the softened butter and granulated sugar until light and fluffy.
- Beat in the eggs, one at a time, until well combined.
- Mix in the milk, vanilla extract, and lemon zest (if using).
- Gradually add the dry ingredients to the wet ingredients, mixing until just combined. Be careful not to overmix.
- Fold in the poppy seeds and lemon juice (if using).

3. Bake the Loaf:

- Pour the batter into the prepared loaf pan and smooth the top.
- Bake in the preheated oven for 50-60 minutes, or until a toothpick inserted into the center of the loaf comes out clean and the top is golden brown.

- Allow the loaf to cool in the pan for about 10 minutes before transferring it to a wire rack to cool completely.

4. Prepare the Glaze (Optional):

- While the loaf is cooling, make the glaze by whisking together the powdered sugar and lemon juice (or milk) until smooth and thin enough to drizzle.
- Once the loaf is completely cool, drizzle the glaze over the top.

5. Serve and Store:

- Slice and serve the loaf once the glaze has set.
- Store any leftovers in an airtight container at room temperature for up to 4 days. The loaf can also be refrigerated for up to a week or frozen for up to 3 months; thaw before serving.

This poppy seed loaf is wonderfully soft and flavorful, with a delicate crumb and a delightful poppy seed crunch. Enjoy it with a cup of tea or coffee for a delightful treat!

Hazelnut Coffee Cake

Ingredients

For the Cake:

- 1 ½ cups (190g) all-purpose flour
- 1 cup (200g) granulated sugar
- 1 tsp baking powder
- ½ tsp baking soda
- ¼ tsp salt
- ½ cup (115g) unsalted butter, softened
- 2 large eggs
- 1 cup (240ml) sour cream or Greek yogurt
- 1 tsp vanilla extract
- 1 cup (120g) finely ground hazelnuts (can be pre-ground or ground yourself)

For the Streusel Topping:

- ½ cup (50g) all-purpose flour
- ½ cup (100g) granulated sugar
- ¼ cup (50g) unsalted butter, cold and cut into small pieces
- ½ cup (60g) finely chopped hazelnuts
- 1 tsp ground cinnamon

For the Glaze (optional):

- 1 cup (120g) powdered sugar
- 2-3 tbsp milk or coffee to thin

Instructions

1. Preheat the Oven:

- Preheat your oven to 350°F (175°C). Grease and flour a 9-inch (23 cm) round cake pan or a 9x9-inch (23x23 cm) square pan, or line it with parchment paper.

2. Prepare the Streusel Topping:

- In a medium bowl, combine the flour, granulated sugar, and ground cinnamon.
- Cut in the cold butter using a pastry cutter or your fingers until the mixture resembles coarse crumbs.
- Stir in the finely chopped hazelnuts. Set aside.

3. Prepare the Cake Batter:

- In a large bowl, cream together the softened butter and granulated sugar until light and fluffy.
- Beat in the eggs, one at a time, until well combined.
- Mix in the vanilla extract.
- In a separate bowl, whisk together the flour, baking powder, baking soda, and salt.
- Gradually add the dry ingredients to the wet ingredients, alternating with the sour cream, beginning and ending with the dry ingredients. Mix until just combined.
- Fold in the finely ground hazelnuts.

4. Assemble the Cake:

- Pour the batter into the prepared cake pan and spread it evenly.
- Sprinkle the streusel topping evenly over the batter.

5. Bake:

- Bake in the preheated oven for 35-45 minutes, or until a toothpick inserted into the center of the cake comes out clean and the top is golden brown.
- Allow the cake to cool in the pan on a wire rack for about 10 minutes before transferring it to the wire rack to cool completely.

6. Prepare the Glaze (Optional):

- While the cake is cooling, make the glaze by whisking together the powdered sugar and milk (or coffee) until smooth and thin enough to drizzle.
- Once the cake is completely cool, drizzle the glaze over the top.

7. Serve and Store:

- Slice and serve the cake once the glaze has set.
- Store any leftovers in an airtight container at room temperature for up to 4 days. The cake can also be refrigerated for up to a week or frozen for up to 3 months; thaw before serving.

This hazelnut coffee cake is rich, nutty, and has a delightful crumb with a crunchy streusel topping. It's perfect for breakfast, brunch, or as a special treat with your afternoon coffee or tea. Enjoy!

Eggnog Macarons
Ingredients:

For the Macaron Shells:

- 1 cup (100 g) almond flour
- 1 3/4 cups (200 g) powdered sugar
- 1/4 cup (50 g) granulated sugar
- 3 large egg whites (room temperature)
- 1/4 tsp cream of tartar
- 1/4 tsp vanilla extract
- 1/4 tsp nutmeg
- A pinch of salt

For the Eggnog Buttercream Filling:

- 1/2 cup (1 stick, 115 g) unsalted butter (room temperature)
- 1 1/2 cups (190 g) powdered sugar
- 2 tbsp eggnog (store-bought or homemade)
- 1/4 tsp vanilla extract
- 1/4 tsp ground nutmeg
- Optional: A pinch of cinnamon

Instructions:

1. **Prepare the Baking Sheets:**
   - Line two baking sheets with parchment paper or silicone baking mats.
   - If you like, you can use a template to ensure your macarons are evenly sized.
2. **Sift Dry Ingredients:**
   - In a bowl, sift together almond flour and powdered sugar. This step helps prevent lumps and ensures a smooth batter.
3. **Make the Meringue:**
   - In a clean, dry bowl, beat the egg whites with cream of tartar and a pinch of salt until they form soft peaks.
   - Gradually add the granulated sugar, a little at a time, while continuing to beat until stiff, glossy peaks form.
   - Gently fold in the vanilla extract and nutmeg.
4. **Combine Ingredients:**
   - Fold the sifted almond flour and powdered sugar mixture into the meringue. Be gentle but thorough, scraping from the sides of the bowl and folding until the mixture flows smoothly off the spatula in ribbons.
5. **Pipe the Macarons:**
   - Transfer the batter to a piping bag fitted with a round tip. Pipe small circles (about 1.5 inches in diameter) onto the prepared baking sheets. Tap the baking sheets on the counter to release any air bubbles and help the macarons settle.

6. **Let Them Rest:**
   - Allow the macarons to sit at room temperature for 30-60 minutes, or until a skin forms on the surface. This helps them develop the signature "feet."
7. **Bake:**
   - Preheat your oven to 300°F (150°C). Bake the macarons for 15-20 minutes, rotating the baking sheets halfway through for even baking. The macarons should be firm to the touch and easily lift off the parchment.
8. **Cool:**
   - Let the macarons cool completely on the baking sheets before removing them.
9. **Make the Buttercream Filling:**
   - Beat the butter until creamy. Gradually add powdered sugar, mixing well after each addition.
   - Add the eggnog, vanilla extract, nutmeg, and optional cinnamon, and beat until smooth and creamy. Adjust the consistency with more powdered sugar or eggnog if needed.
10. **Assemble the Macarons:**
    - Pair up the macaron shells by size. Pipe a small amount of eggnog buttercream onto the flat side of one shell and gently press the matching shell on top to form a sandwich.
11. **Age:**
    - For the best flavor and texture, let the assembled macarons age in the refrigerator for 24-48 hours before serving. This helps the flavors meld and the filling to soften the shells.

Enjoy your eggnog macarons! They're perfect for holiday gatherings or a special treat anytime.

Printed in the USA
CPSIA information can be obtained
at www.ICGtesting.com
CBHW080759240924
14613CB00084B/827